Inherited Secrets

Cynthia Readnower

I have tried to recreate events, locales and conversations from my memories of them or from those passed down from my family, as well as factual newspaper articles. In order to maintain anonymity in some instances, I have changed the names of individuals and places or I may have changed some identifying characteristics and details.

INHERITED SECRETS
Cynthia Readnower

Published by Skinny Leopard Media, Sarasota, FL

Copyright© 2013 by Cynthia Readnower
Photographs Copyright© 2013 by Cynthia Readnower
All rights reserved.

This book, or parts thereof, may not be reproduced in any form without permission, except in the case of brief quotations embodied in critical articles or reviews. The scanning, uploading, and distribution of this book via the Internet or any other means without permission of the publisher is illegal, and punishable by law. Please purchase only authorized electronic editions, and do not participate in or encourage piracy of copyrighted materials. Your support of the author's rights is appreciated.

Library of Congress Control Number: 2013916865
ISBN: 978-0-9899893-1-2

Dedication

Thank you to the people in my life who have shown faith in me and encouraged me. You are truly a gift! To my sons who have taught me so much about life and love, I wish you both joy and happiness.

I have tried to make this book as factual as possible. For those events in the distant past, I have fictionalized some of the remembrances passed down from my family. In a few circumstances, names have been changed to protect those still living.

Prologue

The questioner's emotional voice filled the packed caucus room while he pointed and leaned forward, demanding answers from the man on the "hotseat." Women in wide brimmed hats, some young, some from the upper echelons of Eastern society listened intently while men in suits held their fedoras in their laps.

Reporters hastily scribbled notes and the stenographer's hands flew over the keys, taking in the testimony. Huge movie cameras on six-foot-tall wooden tripods rolled continually, recording everything for posterity. Bulbous microphones stood in front of the committee members and the man in the spotlight. The man, whom everyone focused their attention on, was dressed nattily in a well-cut expensive suit and he had a well-groomed, dark mustache with his hair slicked back fashionably. His face was famous.

The gavel pounded and the questioner asked the man if he would produce the requested witness. "No, I don't think I will," he replied. The questioner, angrier and louder, asked if he would *try* to produce the witness. "No, I don't think I will," the man repeated.

The rapid fire back and forth exchange would command the attention of a nation. It would send ripples of a backlash far and wide and pull in those who had no notion of what was to come. Those participants would soon know notoriety and lose their anonymity. And it all started with the focus of a country on the man known as Howard Hughes.

Chapter 1: Setting the Stage

I know just what those Kewpie dolls in the circus midway feel like. You know those ugly stuffed ones with the painted faces that you throw baseballs at, and they just keep popping back up until you whack them down again? It's *really* hard to get them to stay down. Sometimes, they fall back and at the last second bounce right back up, giving you that shot of adrenalin, making you think you've won when you just get disappointed once they stand back up straight. For months, I have been hit with one shock after another and I just keep bouncing back up and getting ready for another hit. I keep thinking that this will be the last one, that calm will once again prevail over my life, but somehow, that just hasn't been the case.

A year ago, I was praying and praying hard for something in my life to break loose. It was as if things were frozen in place and there was no energy moving. You know like in the dead of August and even if you're on the porch where there should be a breeze, the air is heavy with humidity and inactivity. You sweat just staying in one place. So there you go, maybe I did it to myself with all that infernal praying. Never in my wildest imaginings could I have thought up the things that came my way. Maybe, I'm just not very imaginative. I always thought of my family as dull and boring, with no sense of adventure or excitement. Let me tell you, my family was not the kind you see on reality shows nowadays. My family would have put you fast asleep. We were about as exciting as watching paint dry.

Picture this. A small red brick house, perfectly maintained but dull with no sense of style. One of the few good features of the house was a large front window, but my parents decided to make sure the sun wouldn't bother them inside by putting up the ugliest, most tasteless awning in a peach-colored, corrugated fiberglass that should have been outlawed it was so butt ugly. And come on now, even as a little kid I knew you didn't combine dark red and peach. Inside, the furnishings were always "quality," but tasteless. My parents didn't want anything "fancy" and by that I mean anything that was designed to go together, coordinate or anything that would make you say, "Wow." One of the early decorating ideas my parents had was to buy a roll out mural, have my dad make a plain wooden frame for it and paint it yellow, Yes, yellow. It took up the entire wall space above the sofa, probably six to eight feet long. Underneath, my mother made a slipcover for our sofa in an orange print that was loud, garish and offensive to me even as a small child, which was pretty odd, now that I think of all the "neutral" beige and brown things that would fill the house for most of the rest of its years. Dad used to say that he really wanted more color in the house, but Mom nixed that continually.

We had our own little neighborhood plot of land on a street with mostly wood frame homes that my dad always thought of as a "come down" by just being near them. That didn't mean he would move, though. We were surrounded by people who worked hard for a living; a milk delivery driver, a telephone company employee, a fireman, a couple who were teachers, a college coach (they didn't pay them then like they do now), a shoe salesman and, here and there, a few professionals. The professionals were only in the neighborhood to stash away money so that they could eventually buy a big farm or move on up to a custom built home.

There were lots of kids in the neighborhood and we used to hang out together a lot, most of us within four years in age of one another. At night we played "ghost in the graveyard," kind of like hide-and-go-seek in the dark, got kickball tournaments together and even staged a play one summer. We would catch fireflies and see whether we could keep them alive in a jar poked full of holes in the lid while we debated whether this was cruel or not. Whole swarms of us would ride our bikes together and visit the nearby shopping centers or parks. There were great public swimming pools and if you had a friend that worked for one of the biggest companies in the area, you got into their recreation area with the biggest pool, a river with canoes and lots of trails and cool stuff. They even had a concession stand with chocolate soft serve ice cream.

My dad always went to work in a suit and tie and told us not to let anyone know how much money he made (not that we really knew either). I thought he just didn't want to make anyone jealous because we were "comfortable" and not struggling. I learned years later that because of my dad working for the federal government that my mother had to sever all ties to her aunts, uncles and cousins back in Eastern Europe. This was the era of the "cold war" and my mother could easily be a liability to my father if the government realized that correspondence was flowing across the ocean. I wondered what price that exacted on my mother. Once the Berlin Wall came down and the Russians no longer had a stronghold into those smaller Baltic countries, my mother was free to send care packages to her cousins and correspond with them.

My mom stayed home, cleaned the house a lot, cooked and read her detective novels and watched TV. A very ordinary, routine life. A very rare vacation now and then when we were *very* little and then nothing as we got older. Dinner out at Frisch's once a year. Dull, boring, suffocating.

A big time was watching the traffic come down our street as the government offices let out for the day in the complex at the end of our neighborhood and they used our street to cut through to the larger thoroughfares. For about twenty minutes a day, we were exposed to other people, if just driving by in their cars. One summer, my brothers and their friends hid in the bushes and jumped out with squirt guns to shoot at cars. Unfortunately, a convertible drove by; the driver slammed on the brakes and started to open his door. That was enough to make us scatter far and wide and we all hid for hours.

I watched other kids' parents save all year to have a vacation and be so excited to get away and drive to who knows where. I saw my friends go out to dinner and, once in a while, an expensive restaurant to celebrate milestones. I knew people that joined clubs and had social activities, parties, and dances. I had friends whose parents were thrilled to finally buy a Cadillac or enjoy a lobster dinner. As I got older and went to larger schools, I was exposed to kids whose families owned successful businesses and had huge homes with pools, housekeepers and luxuries. Their lives seemed so glamorous to me. And it wasn't just that they had these things, it was that it was okay to even *want* these things. I was getting the message from my parents to never, ever forget my place.

My family seemed so lifeless. My parents never set any goals, never seemed to "want" or desire anything other than their routine existence. I don't remember seeing them hold hands, share a kiss or even a hug except in extreme circumstances. It was as though someone had wrung the life out of them.

But now, confronted by the secrets I have come to know, maybe that view is bit narrow. Maybe they, and I mean my family and the many that came before me including grandparents, uncles and aunts, just got so used to keeping secrets that everything turned into one. Maybe they just got worn out from all they did when they were young and decided to close themselves off into some sort of protection zone, like a bird protecting its nest. Maybe by the time I came along, the past was buried in so many secrets; no one visited that place anymore. Perhaps the burden of keeping secrets is what made them cling to a dull routine, it was safer that way. Could it be that what they went through made them long for someplace to just hide and live out their days in peace and silence?

Now, the secrets just keep coming. Didn't they all realize that it would come back to haunt everyone, especially the children and their children? Part of me wants to crawl into the darkest corner of my mind and keen with sorrow. The other part of me wants to stand up and cry and scream about all the covering up that's been done and defiantly shout everything to the world so it's out there in the open for once and for all. Let people judge, let people look at us with disdain. My anger knows no bounds, but it's also wrapped up in hurt, wounded so deeply because I was lied to and betrayed and most of all, not found trustworthy enough for my own parents to open themselves up to me and whisper their secrets, knowing that I would treat them gently and not shout them to the world. I would have treated those secrets like something sacred and special, a bond formed between us for the sharing. We would have sat together and talked until the midnight clock struck its mournful sound and shared a magic moment of closeness.

Would I have done things differently if I had been in their shoes? I fervently hope so. I know that in telling this, the secrets stop here. The next generation will know easily and freely the sins of their forefathers and learn to forgive, or at least they will have an option. No waiting until they reach middle age and hitting them with a whammy, no just casually leaving a small clue lying around that would lead step by step to one disclosure and surprise after another. I know that every family has a skeleton or two in the closet, there are those that have a mad old lady hidden in the attic or drinking mimosas on the wraparound porch as they do in the South. (The South knows how to flaunt *their* crazies.) But this was something much more insidious, ranging from murder to a scandal so far reaching that it even touched the White House and Hollywood. And me? I'm just a Midwestern girl that grew up in the "land of values."

Dear Mom,

Last night I dreamed that you were the housekeeper come to take care of the old house and clean it up. Since you are gone and departed, my dream self knew it couldn't really be you but only a "lookalike," a strange moment of lucidity in a mirage. But the pain of seeing you and the longing I had in my heart to hold you once again and lay my head on your shoulder was powerful. You were so perfectly you. You did that little dance step you used to do when you were happy, which wasn't that often. You also did that teasing tone of voice when things were going well. I awoke with tears on my cheeks. I know nothing I can say now will change things, but I wish that I could ask you for just one more conversation. There's so much yet to be said.

It must have been hard for you to be married to Dad so long while he grew insensitive to who you were and what you needed, someone so willing to replace you less than two months since you've been gone. I don't think your needs were ever met or even recognized. No wonder you acted a little crazy at times. Didn't you think you could trust the rest of us with your feelings, didn't you know that we would have been gentler with you? It hurts to realize you didn't believe you could help us to understand why you did the things you did. Now, seeing not only the insensitivity of Dad but his total lack of understanding of how his actions affect others, I wonder if there is something in the gene pool that has missed us, some essential element that allows every human to love and that some of us just don't get.

There seems to be a tradition of emotional abuse, neglect, overuse of power and even murder. What a legacy! It makes me want to hold onto my children with my arms wrapped tightly around them and infuse them with my love, to beg them to understand I'm not like my forefathers. I will love them unconditionally and forever. Can they feel it? Do they know the depths of my heart? The legacy of the past is theirs also. I have already told them the secrets so they will be able to understand people and their darkest fears and actions, so my children will never be knocked unaware of how people, even those you dearly love, can behave. Do they understand?

I know your hand was at my back when the psychic told me about everything. She was able to provide enough validation that I knew the truth in what she said. God forgive me for not recognizing what was going on all these years. Maybe, just maybe I could have helped. Perhaps it is too late now.

Love,
Your daughter, in turmoil

Chapter 2: The Story of Anna and James, Circa. 1906

The First Secret: Murder

It was late in the afternoon when Anna saw the carriage drive briskly through town from her view at the window. Even though most of the carriages looked alike, she could tell by the smart horse and the pace of the driver that it was James. Automobiles had failed to reach this inner rural area yet. He was tall and dressed better than most of the farmers of the district, not that he was rich, but he was the wealthiest in the area. He had land, and land was the soul of the town. He was also lucky in the "looks" department, too; tall, slender and muscular with a headful of thick hair. He had that woman with him again, Hattie. It made Anna's blood boil to see them together. James would turn to look at Hattie in a special, sensual way and Anna would long to rip her eyes out. The jealously in Anna was incredibly strong.

James and Anna had grown up together, being some kind of very distant cousins, although James was several years older. In the small country town, everyone was distantly related to the other anyway and they all knew each other's business. James was a hellion. By the age of fifteen, he was carousing with the older women, charming them, smoking (it was tobacco country after all) and he knew how to handle a horse with power. James was all about power. It oozed out of his pores. If he had grown up in the city, he probably would have headed up a gang. But here, people learned early to stay clear out of his way. He had a dangerous reputation and Anna was just fascinated, and perhaps a bit overconfident, at her ability to "handle" him.

James had married fairly young. That was a surprise to all; however, a child came along very soon. That would be enough to start people talking, except people watched their tongues when it came to James and not many openly said anything about him. It was done in whispers. But his wife died in childbirth and the child was sent to James' parents to raise. James rarely had much to do with the girl. His parents were devout Southern Baptists, no dancing, no card playing, no color in their lives. You might wonder how James ended up being the antithesis of this, but sometimes restrictions make rebellion strong. The girl grew up with the traditions of the church and she grew up bitter, restricted and feeling unloved.

James used to pay Anna just enough attention to keep her interested; he was good at that. Many of the women were in awe of James and the rest were afraid. James didn't bother much with those he had to work at but he did like something of a challenge. Anna had gone on with her own life after James married, even after his wife died. She found a safe man, one who idolized her and wanted only the best for her. He was dedicated to her and also a bit boring. That's why as she watched out the window and spied James' carriage, she still felt that surge of jealousy. The baby stirred in the cradle beside her. She looked briefly over at Bernie's crib and then back to the window. That damn woman, Hattie, made her so mad. She stomped her foot, being careful not to make too much noise to disturb the baby.

Later in the year, the news quickly spread that Hattie had become engaged to a man and it was not James. Anna's satisfaction was quiet but complete. Hah, Hattie would not have him after all. Anna knew she could not have him either but at least another woman was not enjoying him.

The next year passed. Anna occasionally saw James about the town and continued to be polite to him and flirt whenever possible. She might lower her eyes demurely and then raise them to look boldly into his. He would always give her a knowing smile.

James' former girlfriend, Hattie, was soon pregnant and gave birth to a son. She seemed a somewhat distant mother and soon had help to take care of the child. Her husband was able to afford it for her and she took advantage of it. A woman must have children but it didn't have to be too much work. She was able to socialize and be out and about soon. Within the next year she gave birth to another son. People soon realized, however, that this son looked nothing like the first. This son grew fast and tall and soon resembled James. The town had no doubts as to the father of this boy but because of who the father *was*, they kept their mouths shut and even the whispers were few. James showed no knowledge that he was the father. He didn't visit openly and didn't give Hattie any support. Hattie's husband was in a tight spot. If he confronted Hattie, he would also have to confront James' temper and who knew what would happen? So, he kept his head down and soon it was apparent that James was still involved with Hattie for another child, again a boy, was born. It was exceedingly clear that the third boy was the second boy's brother. The town was shocked and silent. Anna was livid. Hattie's husband sold his land and took his wife as far away as possible.

Anna was pleased with her figure. She had regained her slim appearance since Bernie's birth. She dressed carefully and went into town to the general store. She knew, based on routine, that James would likely be coming for supplies soon. She had her back to the door but knew when he entered. It was if some sort of string was pulling her from behind, some type of force that let her know James had come in the door. He said nothing at first, but stood noting her figure and the confidence apparent in her posture. Having a child had made her more of a woman. He liked a woman with hips. Her dark red hair shone with its waves.

"Hello, Anna," he drawled.

She turned and acted surprised. "Well, hello, James," she replied with a slight smile. And then she used all her willpower to turn back around and ignore him when she would rather be staring into his blue eyes. It worked, James was taken aback. If only she could see his face. After a moment he tried again, asking her polite questions until she finally gave him her attention and he gave her his slow lazy smile, one full of awareness.

Later, when Anna would be locked in a passionate embrace with James in a stolen moment, she would wonder what she had started. Where was this going? James was not a man content with just kisses. He urged her to be alone with him. When she was with James, the passion was almost overwhelming, but when she was back home, reason began to set in and she worried about her future. Her husband would look at her reflectively and ask her what was the matter. She knew for her own survival she must get out of this funk. She would then charm her husband and tell him it was just a silly mood. Being the age of men, he didn't think much more about it.

Her husband thoughtfully suggested they have a New Year's party to liven up their routine. They would decorate the house, invite all their friends and dance and sing the night away. Anna was excited even though worry stood in the background. When her husband showed her the guest list he had composed, and told her that he had already invited the men, she almost choked. There on the list was James' name. When she next met James, she begged him not to attend. She used every tactic she could think of to convince him not to show up. But he was too intrigued, this promised to be a great game.

The night of the party, Anna was almost sick with the worry of what might happen. She would have to keep the men apart; there was no doubt about it. She enlisted the aid of one of her girlfriends who reluctantly agreed to be a part of her scheme.

Her friend would keep watch and let Anna know what was going on, as Anna would be busy as hostess. Close to midnight, Anna began to breathe easier. Nothing eventful had happened and the guests were getting louder as the drinking increased. Everyone was laughing, flirting and singing drinking songs. She went to the second floor sitting room, opened the window and mopped her brow. A shadow stood in the doorway and she turned quickly. It was James, obviously having imbibed heavily. He staggered slightly as he crossed over to her and quickly grabbed her and put his hands on her behind, pulling her to him roughly.

"James, no...." she whispered imploringly, "Go back downstairs, you can't be seen here!"

"No", he answered firmly and brought his mouth down to hers opening her mouth with his tongue. She tried to push him away but he had a grip of iron on her. His hands proceeded to paw her. He was rough and thorough in his touch. At another time she would have been thrilled but here in her own home, a home she shared with another man, she was scared and knew she played with fire. To cross over the line so completely was not acceptable and she was scared.

Before James could begin to work his way underneath Anna's clothing, another voice shouted from the doorway. It was Anna's husband, incensed beyond measure. He didn't stop to think about James' size or reputation but charged into the room and grabbed James from behind, shouting and cursing him all the while. He was the smaller man with little experience in hand to hand fighting. It was his outrage that kept him going. Anna was thrown to the wall and stood pressed against it in morbid fear as her husband and James fought brutally. It was obvious within minutes that James was much the stronger. He picked up Anna's husband by his lapels and hurtled him to the floor. Her husband lay there, stunned. It was over, Anna thought, the fight and her life as she knew it. James stood over the man, with blood dripping from cuts on his face, breathing heavily. He looked at Anna with a depth in his eyes like the Devil. She was chilled. Then, Anna watched in slow motion as James picked up her husband, pulled him over his shoulders like a dead weight and walked to the open window. He glanced back at Anna once and then heaved her husband out the window.

Anna stood there in shock as James crossed over to her and started to pull her to him. He stiffened when he realized two people stood in the doorway with their mouths agape and their hands raised as if in protest. One of them was Anna's friend, the one who was supposed to issue the warning. The other was the friend's boyfriend. They would never forget what they had seen. James let go of Anna and strode out the door and out of the house. People were gathered on the lawn around the lifeless body of Anna's husband, all looking up at the window in puzzlement and shock. They watched James purposefully stride away from the house.

The police issued a warrant for James. They didn't look too hard for him for they figured he would turn up. After all, his land was still here and so was his work. He did show up, acting as though everything was normal. He spent some time in jail but at his trial, the witnesses refused to show up. Word was out that they had left the county. Anna testified that she had not seen anything. No one else was called as a witness. James smiled at Anna from his chair.

Months later, Anna and James were married. A single mother couldn't make life work for her in those days. James didn't make Anna send her little Bernie away, but he also didn't like having him around. It was a reminder that Anna had belonged to another man once and that didn't sit well with James. After Anna gave birth to James' daughter and then James' son, she hoped that James would at least accept Bernie. However, once Bernie was twelve years old, James was so hard on him that Anna feared for him. James would beat him for the most inoffensible things. Finally, Anna knew he would kill him one day and sent Bernie away to live with her sister. Bernie would grow up never forgiving her or James and would one day become the ally of James' forgotten daughter, seeking restitution.

Anna became very adept at acting as though nothing was wrong. She carried on, spoiled her Thomas and Mildred and avoided James' wrath. She shared his bed, made his dinner, and did his bidding. He would only hit her if he had been drinking and had a bad day. Otherwise, he seemed proud of her and his children, more so of Thomas because he was the male child.

James took a job in the city and rose to be a regional manager of an insurance company and was one of the few men of his day who knew the value of a good insurance policy. He often traveled. That provided a respite for Anna and the children. She loved her children and she was especially close with Thomas. Both were exceedingly bright and finished high school at a young age, even for those days. Mildred, nicknamed "Mid," finished high school at fifteen and wanted to go on to college. James thought it was a waste and told her he would not pay for it. Mid succeeded in receiving a full college scholarship and never forgave her father for not supporting her. Anna saw Bernie whenever possible but over time she replaced him in her heart with Mid and Thomas.

When Thomas was about sixteen, James was sitting in the living room casually cleaning a shotgun. Every household had guns; it was a way of life. Thomas was in a back room when he heard the gunfire and ran into the living room. His father quickly and quietly wrapped a cleaning cloth around his blood soaked hand and told Thomas to fetch an ambulance. Thomas did not know the extent of the injury but saw the deadly calm on his father's face. He ran the short block to the store where there was a telephone and then ran back home. His father was sitting on the floor where he had left him. James told Thomas to get some more towels and wrapped them around his hand. Once the ambulance took James away, Thomas proceeded to clean up the blood left behind. It was not apparent until later that James had blown away his hand in the accident. It never hindered James, because the disability insurance policy had him set up for life. He never had to work again. The official story was that the trigger of the shotgun got caught on the strap of a pair of overalls that James had been wearing. And as for the gun, Thomas had left it there, loaded, the guilt almost unbearable for him to carry in the years that followed. No one seemed to question why someone so used to guns in their lives wouldn't think to check if it was loaded or not before cleaning it.

Thirty years later, James' grandchildren would remark on a picture where James was standing with Anna proudly showing his handless arm to the camera. What kind of man would do that, his grandchildren wondered.

Chapter 3: The Discovery

My aunt Mid explained that she knew this story and always had. My father, Thomas, claimed he didn't know. Years ago, among my father and aunt, there was small talk with me about this, but when the Internet made everything available it was possible to find out that my grandfather James had indeed been tried for the murder of my grandmother Anna's first husband. After being acquitted, my grandmother and grandfather moved to Indiana to escape the notoriety. They were both extradited back to Kentucky to stand trial again and my grandmother was also charged. They were both acquitted, again, due to the absence of witnesses.

My grandmother's first husband, Arthur, was killed on June 27, 1910. She married my grandfather soon after and gave birth to my aunt in 1912 and my father in 1917. I never got to meet my grandfather, known as "Grandad" to all, since he died of a heart attack around the age of seventy, just before I was born. My grandmother lived a quiet life as I was growing up, with her life centered on her friends in the neighborhood, her church, and taking in college students as boarders. The boarders lived in the upstairs bedrooms and my grandmother would cook breakfast for them.

I loved her old house, and when there weren't any boarders, we were allowed to go up the winding, mahogany staircase and see the rooms. Even in those days, it seemed very old fashioned with heavy, dark furniture, rose patterned carpets and white, embroidered doilies adorning the furniture tops. What impressed me was the stillness of it all, as if someone had just up and vanished and left everything in place, never to return.

My mother and grandmother had some friction between them. During our frequent visits to Kentucky, I remember my grandmother as being opinionated and prejudiced. My mother would often explain my expected behavior to me for our time there and I tried to play my part as a respectful, quiet granddaughter.

I remember being taken down the street one time to a neighbor and standing on her porch as my grandmother introduced us and the neighbor inspected me. The woman had a heavy, German accent and never invited us inside. They discussed me as if I weren't even there.

Dear Mom,

I think about your illness and how at the end you never cried, never mourned for yourself and told me that you were complete, you had a wonderful life and a wonderful family. Grace and dignity. I am overwhelmingly proud of how you handled the end. The strength you showed in your acceptance is a shining example. Would I have been able to do the same?

The events that have taken place since you passed have shown me that you were the glue holding the family together. It makes me wonder if you were behind every good deed within our house. Did our father even think about us in that same way, about what we needed emotionally? What you must have suffered knowing the past the way you did. I know you must have felt guilt, remorse and also regret. You must also have felt that there was no changing it and decided to carry on even if you were much less than happy. I knew you were sad; I tried to be the one to make you happy but failed. I can see now that there was so much more involved, so much that could never be said. The only way that you could be complete is to change the past, which is impossible.

I coped with losing you by thinking you had gone to a better place and your spirit was free. While I still believe that, I also wonder about what you would want me to do, how to live my life differently. It has given me a sense of renewal in ways, a sense of commitment to myself to not waste any more time. I am determined not to suffer the way you did. I also see that some of the things you did were actually driven out of strength when at the time, I thought it was denial of reality. Many of the thoughts of my childhood, the intuition I felt about certain things, have come back to haunt me. I really was right at the time. There is a coldness being passed down in the genes, a haunting, frightening cold.

Love,
Your daughter, the "martyr"

The Scene

He sat in an elegantly upholstered chair, looking relaxed and loosely holding a science magazine in his lap. His dark blond hair was slicked back from his face showing his high forehead, broad nose and a wide smile. He looked friendly and slightly goofy. His dark suit sported a white pocket-handkerchief that matched his perfectly starched white shirt. The patterned tie combined dark and light to be the perfect complement. Behind him was a floor lamp with its white silk shade and draperies flowed to the right of the chair.

She sat on the arm of the chair, lightly gripping her right thumb with her left hand, as though she were trying to keep her hands from moving in her lap. The exposed forearms showed a delicate watch with a narrow black band and a bracelet of stones on the other. A wedding ring was evident. Her thick, dark locks were pulled off her face and pinned above the ears, so that cascades of jet-black waves flowed down to her shoulders. Her conservative but stylish dress was also dark, tucked in at the waist with a slim belt and the sleeves were very slightly puffed at the shoulders. A necklace of dark stones completed her ensemble. She smiled at the cameras, too, although her bright smile of perfect teeth might have portrayed many things. One could interpret it as the smile of a beautiful woman or the expression of someone who knows a secret, perhaps the slightest bit smug.

Flashbulbs snapped and the photograph was sent to the news wire agencies to be featured on front pages everywhere. If given a photo op, you might as well make the best of it, even in the worst of circumstances.

Chapter 4: Forgiving, Not Forgetting

I did a lot of work a few years back, trying to forgive all the people (and especially my parents) in my life for any wrongs, real or imagined, committed against me. I read a lot of self help books and talked to people who knew about what forgiveness meant. You see I never really felt accepted as a child. I felt the expectations of who and what my parents wanted out of me but very little acceptance of who I was as a person. Oh, poor baby, you may be saying wryly. The feelings I just described also belong to a few other hundred million children in this world. Ours was not the generation of "free love" no matter what everyone cried; ours was the generation of rebellion and trying to change the world. Our parents'generation was based on survival, pure and simple, a roof, food and clothing, not self-actualization. So...my problem also belongs to countless millions, but it hurt nonetheless.

I guess I could have just seen a therapist and tried to work through things that way, but I'm not really a traditional person. So when realizing I had to forgive my parents for my own self-preservation, I did something called Rohun. I worked with a practitioner that had me lie on a massage table and then she did some relaxation and visualization work. The crux of the matter was that you remember scenes that have bothered you and then you consciously make a choice to forgive the people who caused you pain by seeing the scene float up to the sky on a cloud and just keep letting go until you can no longer visualize it. If the cloud just won't go, or falls back to Earth then you're not ready to forgive. The practitioner told me that by changing my own energy, I could change relationships. Not quite a believer, I did a few of these sessions and didn't really notice anything until about six months later.

After I did that work, a change really did take place. I began to feel loved and appreciated by my parents. The little digs that would come out of my parents' mouths ceased and were replaced with compliments. Wow, this stuff really worked. Or maybe everyone was mellowing with age, but I did begin to have a relationship with my parents based on love. I decided also that since they were aging and had started out as older parents anyway, that I would never leave unfinished business concerning them. So... I wrote them at least once a week and made sure we talked often. I tried to look at it that when I did get to visit them I would be grateful they were still here, still here in the flesh to hug and talk to. It made the idiosyncrasies easier to deal with. I made sure never to forget any special occasions. My mother truly was a wonderful grandmother to my children, a much better grandmother than she was a mother. They had a special relationship with her based solely on love from the start. She was kind and generous with them and openly playful. She would not tire of the games they played and would send them little surprises. She would hug them and tell them she loved them in such an open way that I marveled how she had changed. They loved her back, so totally and openly and were so accepting of her. It was beautiful.

Knowing now what I do, I wonder what exactly stopped my mother from letting me know what went on in her past. It must have been so painful for her to live with it and not discuss it. She told me that she absolutely longed for a daughter and when she got pregnant with me, just intuitively knew I would be a girl.

In the end years, she would allude mysteriously to something she wanted to tell me. She would look distressed (I chalked it up to melodrama) and give me enough information to let me know that some event in the past, shadowy and dark, concerned my aunt (my father's sister) and uncle and my father. She always said she would tell me this "something" after my father had passed. Everyone just assumed she would live the longest since she hardly ever got sick.

She had few female friends. There were only two that I remember her talking about with fondness. One, I remember visiting as a little girl. She was a spinster and lived with her cousin whose husband had died. She was sweet and gentle. The women dressed as in days gone by, very prim and proper and never wore pants. The other friend of my mother's I never met although my mother corresponded with her over the years but never had a "heart to heart" talk with her that I know of.

My mother was blessed with brothers, no sisters, and was not especially close with her mother so there was no one she shared her heart with. I did get bits and pieces over the years but never the real, whole story. She even withdrew from her brothers and their families. At the time I believed it was because my father was a bit anti-social with her family and so being together was more a worry for my mother than a pleasure, but now I wonder if it was because they also knew the secrets and she could never feel comfortable around them. Perhaps they had judged her or made their feelings known. That would have pushed her away. But what scares me the most is that I wonder what if she saw a bit of my father in me and so she never opened up to me because of it. What if the hardness that was in him was also in me and so she closed herself off to me? It makes me ache to think that she would see that in me. I know that it is there but I also know that I have chosen to deny that part of me. I have had ample opportunities to act on it but instead have tried to choose love, not selfishness. But of course, as a young person growing up, as most teenagers are, I judged my parents to be ignorant creatures. But part of my judgment was the way of life my parents had chosen. My father worked, came home from work, read the paper and went to bed. My mother cooked, cleaned, cried and stayed up late to watch television. I used to wish they would divorce rather than live like that. In all our old home movies, my mother would have the camera focused on us and my father would be sitting in his favorite chair reading the paper, totally oblivious to what was going on around him, never participating. Of course, there was more to that than just a situation, it was more a way of life.

    I can remember wanting to play the piano from the age of three. My mother bought me a functioning two-foot tall, toy spinet piano with twenty-four keys when I was about five years old. I had a little stool and sat at the piano and would play by colors that were on a strip of cardboard that sat on top of the keys. The music was also color-coded. I did fairly well at this and by the time I was eight years old, I was dying to play the real thing. I went shopping with my mother and father to look at pianos. My father would look at old battered pianos while my mother and I would cruise the front part of the showroom looking at the new ones. There was a gorgeous piano, a limited centennial edition that sounded like heaven to my ears. Of course, it was too expensive and if we were to get a piano, there was one condition. I was never to play the piano when my father was home because he didn't like the noise and he also felt I would never be any good at it. I agreed to the condition, of course, the need for music was overwhelming to my soul. Anyway, we went home thinking that all the pianos were just too much money. The next week or so, I came home from school and my mother was standing inside the doorway smiling broadly. As I stepped over the threshold I saw the centennial edition piano in our small living room. It was pure joy. I remember that moment as one of the happiest of my life.

    I took lessons from an ex-concert pianist in the old style, strictly classical. By the time I was fourteen, my teacher said she had taught me all that she could and the next step would be the college's Conservatory of Music forty-five minutes away by car. Of course, that would never really be considered because my father would never pay for the cost and the inconvenience of driving every week but I kept my end of the bargain, never playing when he was home and he never asked to hear me play, either.

Dear Mom,

From the time I was small, I always felt there was another person hiding inside of you. When you didn't want to leave the house, didn't want to have any pleasures, refused the automatic dishwasher saying you would rather do it by hand, wouldn't go out to eat, I still had trouble coming to terms with all those things because I saw in you someone carefree and breezy. I didn't understand why you didn't know that person was inside of you. One of my fondest memories is of you sitting in a chair drying your hair next to the fireplace and you were reading a book about newspaper bloopers. You started to giggle and then laughed till tears ran down your cheek. You were as tickled as I have ever seen you. That is the way I thought you should be. I can still remember some of the silly things that had you in stitches, one was a blooper in a church bulletin that had been worded in such a way as to say that all mothers giving milk should plan to donate at the bake sale, but it made it sound that women who were nursing should do it right there. Weird, but you couldn't stop laughing.

My neighbor enjoyed meeting you and I remember you and she stood at the curb between my house and hers and you talked to her for hours. Do you know what she remembers of you? She compared you to a young Katherine Hepburn, carefree with a scarf blowing in the wind. She saw it too, and she didn't even know you. So what prevented you from realizing that person was there? Wouldn't you have been happier letting her out, wouldn't we all?

I know we all have lessons to learn. We wouldn't be here if we didn't but what if we could learn them quicker or with less pain. Would everything have changed if you stood up for yourself, expressed your independence and made us see the woman you were inside? Perhaps you had already tried it and it backfired and that is why I never saw it. Perhaps, since I came along later in your life, the life's blood inside of you was already ebbing away.

Love, Your wistful daughter

Chapter 5: Thomas

There was a picture of Thomas at the age of four in the old fashioned dress of the times, literally a dress for a boy. It was tradition that little boys dressed that way until they received their first set of "knee britches" and from then on that's what they wore. He was a towhead and smiling. Other pictures as he grew would show him with a pony, with a pet goat and with his favorite uncle, his substitute father during the summers.

Thomas moved around a lot as a boy. James, his father, was restless and moved them to and from the city to the country every few years. Anna never protested. She couldn't. Once, their house burned down with Thomas' pet dog inside. The fire was suspicious and happened when the family had gone to church. With James' reputation, perhaps it was payback.

The death of Thomas' beloved pets was a pattern he would experience many times. James would just tell him it was a part of life and especially farm life. A pet goat was trying to reach through a fence to get to the tantalizing leaves on the other side and accidentally hung itself when its horns got caught in the fence. Thomas would never have pets in his adult life nor allow his children to.

Thomas knew never to question his father. At one point when they were living in the country, James and a neighbor had an argument about the water rights on James' property. The neighbor felt it was his right to cross over James' property to get to the water. James got in his buckboard, drove it to the edge of the property and camped out there for three days holding his shotgun. The neighbor ended up apologizing and the water rights were restored.

When Thomas was about ten years old, one of his aunts died and as was the custom of the day, the body was laid out in her home and attended by all the relatives for days. James and Anna left Thomas there and went off on errands. Thomas was outside hanging out with the men when one of them told him to go inside, find the man's wife and ask her to fetch him his pipe. Thomas was a boy and had no choice but to go. He stood in the doorway hoping not to see the dead body. The woman he was meant to see was not there. He edged closer into the room, hugging the walls until finally, as if someone were pulling his head up, he peeked at the coffin and saw his aunt. It struck terror into his heart and he ran from the house. He stayed away the rest of the day until all the people milling around had left for the day, with only the women left inside with their vigil. After dark, his older cousin Imogene came looking for him and told him she would take him home and he could stay the night with her and her husband. He readily went and never really did find out where his parents were and why they had abandoned him there. It was his deepest and fiercest experience of being alone, one he would remember even as an elderly man.

Anna's sister, Rena was married to a tall, mild mannered man everyone just called "Red" because of his thick, gloriously copper colored hair. He was a shy man ideally suited to country life. He raised his own hogs, sheep and crops and lived quietly with Rena. Their one heartbreak was that no children ever came along. They loved children. Thomas was invited to spend the summers with them and was always welcomed with an open heart. It was here that Thomas would understand the meaning of love and what it meant to be a man. Red was tough about work and living with nature, but kind to Thomas and taught him to hunt, ride a horse, and about the land. Thomas was happiest during these summers.

One summer day, Thomas took his pony into the town to get a few items at the general store. On the way back, a dog along the roadside barked at the pony and spooked it. The pony reared and Thomas was on the ground with a bleeding wound in his head. The pony ran on home with Thomas sitting stunned in the middle of the dirt road. When Red saw the pony come home, he immediately knew something was wrong, mounted his own horse and went looking for Thomas. He found him and tended to his cut. It was this kind of thing that would make Thomas love Red with all his heart.

When Thomas was fourteen, he decided to run away to Florida. No matter that he had never been there before or that he had barely even made it out of his own state, it just sounded like a place he wanted to see. He was sick to death of hearing his parents argue. It would start especially after his father had been drinking. Sometimes, it would end with his mother crying or with a smart sound of a slap or even worse. Thomas learned to make himself scarce and not be around if possible. His parents didn't keep track of him too tightly so it was easy for him to go somewhere else. They were too tightly wrapped up within themselves. Thomas made the mistake of boasting to Red about his plan and of course, Red talked him out of it. Red knew the boy wouldn't be able to fend for himself yet and Thomas needed an excuse not to go anyway. He wasn't stupid. For the rest of his life, Thomas would try to avoid conflict when he could not win. However, if he was sure of the outcome, things were different. His own anger was a learned behavior, learned at his father's knee.

James readily agreed to send Thomas to college. He was proud of his boy and knew he was smart. Thomas went away to a good university several hours away. He would send his laundry home, as was the custom of the day, in a leather box designed just for the purpose. Anna would wash, iron and starch his shirts and mail them back. When Thomas was able, he would come home for a visit. During one such time, his father was drinking too much and his mother made the mistake of disagreeing with him. She knew her mistake quickly as James' eyes glazed with anger and he charged toward her. Thomas also knew his mother's mistake but this time he was home as a man, not as a boy. He grabbed a wine bottle nearby and caught up to his father and holding the bottle over the man's head, swore to him that he would use it. His father's surprise gave Thomas a feeling of quiet satisfaction. James backed down and stomped out of the house. Thomas would never see James go after his mother again.

Thomas graduated from college with honors and found a job paying a small wage near home. He lived with James and Anna in the city and was barely able to make ends meet. He had to pay for the streetcar, his lunch, his work clothes and help out with expenses at home. After a brief time, James announced that they were moving once again to the country. It would be impossible for Thomas to follow and still hold his job. Thomas found a small room to rent in an old lady's house and started to look for a better paying job. He never did understand why his father chose that particular moment in his life to change residences once again. He felt he was being thrown out on the street and again felt abandoned. If only James could have waited six months.

Thomas gradually worked his way up to better jobs. He moved in with his sister and her husband in another city and was happy with them. Mid harbored no resentment toward her brother and readily helped him. She had done well herself in college and, unlike most of the women of her day, had dedicated herself to a career. She and her husband had decided not to have children, an almost unheard of plan in those days. She was actually quite glamorous when she was young, svelte with luxurious, thick, wavy dark hair and luminous eyes. She could have made a killing in Hollywood in her day.

Thomas' employers appreciated his sharp mind and work ethic. He could cut through the baloney quickly to get to the heart of the matter. He had a good business sense. Thomas was a bit of a loner but willing enough to go out for a drink or get together after work. He was ideally suited for management. He could do his job without worrying about his subordinate's reactions or what they would think of him.

In college, Thomas was no stranger to drinking and smoking and carousing with women. He and his casual buddies would hitch rides for miles to meet up with a few "girls" to drink, dance and flirt or "score." His buddies were more apt to score with the women for Thomas was more reserved. The women who went for him were usually the ones who liked the more silent type. He might have a brief fling with one or two, but nothing serious came of them. One woman that he dated in college, Lydia, continued to stand out in his mind. There were lots of dances and he pinned her one year with his fraternity pin. In those days, the men wore tuxes to fraternity dances and the women wore slinky, silky, backless dresses, as was the style of the 1930s. Very glamorous were the men and women in those days! People still dressed up just to venture downtown. Even after Thomas and Lydia went their separate ways, she being involved in her family's solid business, Thomas kept in touch and would occasionally visit her in the city where she lived. The relationship gradually took on more serious tones but neither one put a lot pressure on the other. Both seemed content to let things coast for a while. Lydia was busy and career minded in her own way. Lydia finally decided to force the issue of marriage and moved to the city where Thomas worked. She began to see him much more often.

When Thomas was twenty-four, he took a job as vice president of a small aircraft products company. Business was booming as the threat of World War II loomed over everyone's heads. Thomas was soon allowed to hire his own bookkeeper and a woman came in one day for an interview. She had no college education but had been working for six years since graduating from high school. She was petite and brunette with the most turquoise eyes that ever existed on the earth and the most ready, but slightly shy smile. Thomas was disappointed to read the "Mrs." in front of her name, Kathryn Weaver. He was instantly attracted to her. He worked alongside her, educating her in the ways of the company and her duties and was pleased to see she was a quick learner. She had a brightness about her that made their time together pleasant. He encouraged her to go take evening classes at the YMCA to learn more about accounting and she did. She followed his advice to the letter, which was a great feeling of power for him.

Chapter 6: Kathryn

One of her first memories was of being alone in the sparely furnished room of a house alongside the railroad tracks. She was not allowed to go outside because of the "hobos" that rode the rails. Who knew what could happen to a small girl with all the men that came through the town in those days, homeless, poverty stricken and desperate. The Depression had created a new class of society, one that really encompassed all classes but you never knew who had been a family man and who was a crook so you had to be careful. There were no toys other than a hand-me-down doll that a distant aunt had given her. She spent her day staring out the window and listening to her mother work in the background baking bread, taking care of the babies, scrubbing. She was called upon to help out in whatever way a five-year old could and she would learn to change diapers before learning to read. At this point, she didn't speak English yet and would have to learn when she entered school. The community was mainly a composition of Eastern European immigrants so English was not so important here. Her father worked in the foundry and her mother didn't believe in banks, so the Depression didn't hit them any harder than anyone else. Whatever money they had was spent on food and shelter. Her father would have spent more on drink except Kathryn's mother always got to the money first and doled it out carefully.

Kathryn was the only girl among four boys. As such, there were different expectations for her. The oldest son was idealized and spoiled. Extra food and candy were given to him because he was to be the future of the family, the salvation. This son grew to be a wild one, attractive to women, but of course that would come later. Kathryn longed to feel her mother's love in this special way, but never would. Instead, she was taught what a woman's place was and at this time in history, it wasn't very hopeful. Kathryn grew weary of hearing her father and mother fight when her father had been drinking. At times, there was screaming and shouting and memories of her mother threatening her father with a knife to stay the hell away from her. Kathryn would grow up dreading conflict because she had her fill of it as a child.

By the age of nine, Kathryn would be sent to the market and learned to negotiate the price of a roast with the butcher. She would take a wagon and haul the meat back home and would account for every penny. Her mother might not have spoken English but knew American money well. On occasion, Kathryn was allowed to buy candy for herself. By the age of twelve she was caring for the youngest brother who idolized her like a second mother. She had to take him everywhere she went and very often resented him as much as she loved him. She was able to pour out much of the affection she held inside when with him, but she also was becoming a young woman and having to watch after him continually was tedious. One day, she intentionally let him walk into a tree without warning him and then felt so guilty; she gave him all her candy for a month. The guilt she felt from that episode changed the way she viewed her responsibility.

In school, Kathryn excelled. It was her escape and she always did her work and studied hard. She tried to read everything she could get her hands on. Her mother tried to make her quit school in high school, to get a job and bring home some money. Kathryn dug her heals in and finished school, something only her youngest brother was also able to do.

After her family had moved to a different neighborhood, Kathryn's saving grace was that a family with five older girls lived next door. At different times, different sisters would befriend her and they were the ones who helped her to choose her clothes, understand boys and get her invited to parties. She was able to escape from her houseful of brothers and know feminine friendship. It was something she would never forget.

There were always lots of young men about the house. The oldest brother was only a year and a half ahead of her, so his friends would eye her when they came to see her brother. For the most part, knowing how her brother often got up to no good, she ignored these attentions. Besides, they only paid attention to her sex, not who she was as a person. When she was eighteen, getting ready to finish high school, she began to notice one of the young men paying her attention but not leering or being disrespectful. He was an acquaintance of her brother, but not a close friend, which was in his favor. With her mother urging her to get a job and pay rent to live in her own house, Kathryn was under pressure to plan out her future. She began to open herself up to the young man's attentions. He had recently broken up with a girlfriend and was ripe for a new relationship, or so she thought. He had a real job working in a factory and was able to afford an apartment. This sounded like heaven to Kathryn. Soon, Kathryn was engaged to him and a wedding day was planned. She was happy; she cared for him and was excited about her new life. She glowed as she took her wedding vows; it was so wonderful to belong to someone.

Dear Mom,

I remember the day that we found out you had been married before. We were going through the genealogy book that Dad's father created before his death and there was an extra last name for you. We questioned that and every adult in the room stood breathless waiting to hear your response. You very sternly told us we would discuss it later and your expression closed off any possibility of discussion right then. Perhaps if you had acted like it was no big deal we wouldn't have keyed into it. However, it was intriguing to us kids. Finally, days later, you told us that you had been married before and that your first husband didn't want kids and so you divorced him. It would be years before it occurred to me that you didn't have kids for eight years after you married Dad. Hardly a rush to get pregnant. I tried to ask a question about it months later and you were so infuriated by it that you told me never to speak of it again. Your anger scared me so badly that I thought that divorce must be one of the most terrifying events in the world. It certainly took the wind out of my sails and I was terribly wounded at your lack of trust in confiding in me. In later years, you would let drop a smattering of facts about your first marriage. From those comments, I construed that perhaps your first husband had abused you, had done terrible damage to your psyche, had in some way made you incapable of loving openly now. You said that he had married you on the rebound so perhaps he had affairs? Perhaps you felt lost and alone? I never asked questions, though, a remnant of that day when you warned me off. Perhaps I should have. I decided that you needed to know you were loved and started my campaign to impress you with *my* love. I would come home from school and sit on your lap and hug and kiss you and tell you that you owned my child's heart. My heart cries now for how hard that child in me tried to help you feel loved.

As you got older, and you showed a distinct lack of trust in my choices, I turned away from you. Do you remember in high school when you lectured me about what my boyfriend must be feeling like when we had an argument and you urged me to give in and apologize to him? You never asked about my side or even found out that he had seen another girl, he was doing drugs and that he had real problems. I was supposed to cave in because *he* might be hurt. Now, it makes sense. Now I understand. It wasn't my situation you were dealing with, it was your past.

Love, Your indignant daughter

Chapter 7: Life Lessons

    Life is a culmination of lessons learned. You can grow up with someone and then one day after knowing them fifty years, find out you don't really know them at all. Unless the right situation comes along and you see that they can be deceitful, dishonest and dishonorable, you may never know what they are truly made of. So life is just a series of events that teach you things and if you learn your lesson fast, you get to move on to another lesson. If you don't learn it, you repeat it over and over. I have come to know that I want the lessons to be taken care of quickly and well, not to repeat them, so I usually analyze situations to see what I am supposed to learn, perhaps overly so.
    I know that I became an overachiever because I was trying so hard to get my parents' approval. Perhaps a healthier way would have been to just not care so much. It would have saved me great anxiety trying to work extra hard and achieve what I thought they wanted, not what I wanted. I easily set myself up for more hurt because I couldn't get their approval, the truth was they didn't have it in them to show me that they approved even if they did. When people are unhappy within themselves they are unlikely to make others happy. Maya Angelou said to "never take a shirt from naked man," meaning that if someone doesn't love themselves, they cannot love *you*.
    You know how certain things stick out in our childhood, the things that have shaped your life? Well, if they don't then you have a bigger problem and that's denial. Anyway, one of the things I remember is the gradual decline of my mother's happiness. If you look at our family pictures before I was nine, my mother would be smiling broadly and looking happily into the camera. After that time, there was a brooding air to my mother, one of a cloud of unhappiness circulating around her. I

still wonder what it was that changed her, something to do with her and my father's relationship. I often wondered if he had an affair then but have never had any proof of it. My mother would get a certain look in her eye and I would know that she was about to start a downward spiral. She would cry, be morose and dinner would usually be sparse and unappetizing. I could barely eat these meals. You can imagine that all three of us kids ended up with some type of eating disorder. Meals around our house were pure misery.

My mother's moods were proof to me that she just didn't love me enough. If she did, then I would be enough for her. Yeah, I know, "kid logic." I knew my father was insensitive to her needs but I wanted to tell her to snap out of it, just stand on your own two feet. I had my own battles to fight, also. When I was fourteen and in junior high, I was assailed by a sudden lack of self-esteem that was so great that I was miserable. I felt unloved and spent hours in my room crying. On top of this, my father chose to harass me with nasty comments such as telling me "I cackled like a hen" when I laughed. Nowadays, psychologists will tell you that the way a father interacts with a daughter at this very delicate time in her life, will shape her destiny and sense of self for the rest of her life. If that weren't enough, my mother was missing in action, wrapped up at this time in her life about sorrows from the past. I didn't have a lot of patience with her at this time. My mother would get strange notions in her head and then act like they were real and sob and cry until my father came home. He would ask what was wrong and then when we would tell him, he would just shake his head and walk away, never addressing the situation.

Finding a boyfriend at the age of fifteen saved my life. I got lots of attention at school and my boyfriend was my salvation. We clung to each other and planned our escapes from our families. At one point, he broke up with me and I think I barely ate for three weeks until he came back asking forgiveness. I don't recall that my parents even noticed or asked where he was. It was as though I were an island amid this mix of unhappy, misbegotten people.

I graduated early from high school and moved out into an apartment before the rest of my class had even exited high school. I was so focused on doing this, that nothing could have held me back. I went to night school for college and worked full time. I became so driven that a one point I actually worked *full* time and went to the university *full* time. Talk about efficient time management! But to do this, something inside me had to give. There were no soft spots left, no easy going laid-back ways. My heart hardened as I drove myself to succeed. I learned to deny that female part of me and used my mother's emotional instability as a reason to do so. Logic and reason were my prevailing forces. I learned to embrace the masculine side of me, at the same time trying to look sexy and attractive. I inwardly saw my relationship with men as proof of my desirability, although simultaneously, I recognized these men were just as hopelessly lost as I was, for they knew me not at all. I was their challenge; I was a prize to be won, not a living breathing human being.

Dear Mom,

Do you remember that one time when my brother was home from college in the summer? You were upstairs and he and I were teasing one another and joking around. He must have been about twenty years old and I was sixteen. It was a lazy, boring day. I was on the basement stairs sitting, and he was standing in the doorway of his room that Dad and he had built in the basement. We were trading insults good-naturedly and generally just passing the time. I said something to him, and he replied tauntingly telling me I better watch what I say or he would show me his "hairy moon." Later, you were involved in one of your crying, moody jags and called me into your bedroom. You asked me what my brother and I had been doing that he could show me his "hairy moon." You were deadly serious. I'm sure my mouth dropped open and a scream escaped my lips for later my brother would tell me he heard me yell loudly and wondered what was the matter. Incest? Is that what you were implying? Jesus Christ, how sick could you be! I ran from the room after telling you that you WERE sick. You would cry the rest of the day and my father would again repeat his performance and ignore the entire situation.

Later, I would hear through the family grapevine and still do not know if this is the absolute truth, that my grandmother had shoved you into a closet with one of your brothers and told you to grope each other to figure out your male and female differences. That was supposedly early sex education. I don't know if you complied and I can't imagine being the only girl in a family of four brothers. What if....?

You told me early on how awful sex was and that a woman took it just to have children. For a while I wondered what was so awful and then the "I think thou dost protest too much" had me intrigued by the whole thing. You talked about it altogether too much. I began to wonder if you were just truly repulsed by the whole thing or if my dad was just an inept lover. It's taken me all my life to truly figure out why you told me this and it didn't have anything to do with either thing. It was a whole different animal entirely.

Love, Your doubting daughter

The Scene

Of all the news stories competing for the headline, it was her face that captured the front page of hundreds of newspapers across the country. It helped that she was movie star photogenic and the story was juicy and scandalous. Her picture in this headline was given to the press by her parents, making sure it was a good one.

Next to her picture was one of her husband just leaving an airplane after a flight from Washington, D.C. Peeking out from behind him was an attractive flight attendant in a uniform with her hat jauntily perched on her head. She was smiling for the camera. The subject of the picture was patting his overcoat or maybe just pulling it closed. It was November after all and the plane was exposed on the runway. He would calmly reply, "No comment," to the reporters, get into an airport cab and leave the municipal airport. The reporters followed him downtown and on to his home.

Other stories of the day, relegated to their secondary position, concerned a woman who died at the age of 81 and left 140 direct descendants, including 64 great grandchildren and seven great-great grandchildren; the death of a German hygienist in a Soviet occupied zone; a baby who suffocated in its crib; and the change of dress code from knickerbockers to suits with long pants for Senate pages who ran errands. The pages were ages 12-16 years old.

At least four other articles centered on her, as well as the title headline. By this time, the tide was turning and sympathy seemed to be going her way. At least, judgment was being passed on the one who had brought her into this, and she appeared to have been wronged.

Chapter 8: Amateur Psychology

There are different degrees of love. Some love is really just needing someone else. True love means wanting someone's happiness before your own. Is the ultimate love sacrificing yourself for someone else? No, it isn't supposed to go that far for then you are admitting that you are valueless and your love would be worthless, too. That is one of life's most difficult lessons. You have to be selfish enough to value yourself, or others won't value you at all.

Dear Mom,

When I used to complain to you about something Dad did, you used to defend him, however, at times you did complain about something he had done to you. It didn't last long, because you acted guilty to be speaking against him. I always thought you defended him because you were united with him. Now I realize you might (just might) have been protecting us. You wanted us to have a good relationship with him and believe he cared for us and so you wouldn't let us think otherwise except when it just leaked out unintentionally. You were willing to stuff down your own feelings, swallow your own bile rather than allow us to realize the truth. The truth was he just didn't have it in him.

I know you had a lack of self-esteem. I could see it in the ways you would let other people have the upper hand and never stick up for yourself. I remember when your sister-in-law said something to you that hurt your feelings; instead of responding you just avoided being in her company for years (and years and years). You also taught us to run away from a battle, never to stand and fight, that nothing was worth it. Now I wonder if that attitude stemmed from childhood or from later in life and the regret at decisions you had made. I used to tell my friends that I was brought up to be a "victim" for I always say that you and Dad wanted us to think that nothing was worth dying for, nothing worth taking a stand for. But it backfired because I grew up to be very rebellious; I still am, but now in a more diplomatic and tactful way. Instead of rabble rousing, I write articles about how to change the world and letters to the editor. So you did your job, just not in the way you expected. I grew up to be a stronger person because of my struggles at home and the constant need to stand up for myself.

Love, Your stronger daughter

Chapter 9: Realization

So what does it take for a person to learn his lesson? At Mom's funeral, my dad refused to leave his private room and greet any of my mother's family, her brothers and their wives, nieces, nephew, etc. He used the reason of not being able to control his emotions and he *did* sob through the entire service. Everyone was very understanding and naturally upset themselves. My father had never really shown any emotion to or for my mother's family other than disdain. They had nothing in common he would say, and it went back to division of the "classes." He went to college, they didn't finish high school. Never mind that all of them were self taught electronic and computer near-geniuses and had assembled their own working computers from spare parts. My dad had nothing to do with them. I think this attitude always kept my mother a bit isolated.

So after the funeral, near Christmas, one of my uncles stopped by to see my dad and brought a fruit basket, a significant gesture. My dad was puzzled by this behavior. One of my dad's mottos in life was that "people are no damn good." Now, my dad had never done anything nice for this man, hardly ever bothered to give him the time of day. Did my dad ever change his attitude after receiving this gift? NO, and that's a HELL NO!

I also wonder what it would take to think that your kids are also part of the "no damn good" part of the world. We have never done anything to hurt him, only been respectful and tried to earn his love. But his attitude has never changed and even after having three great high achieving kids and several grandchildren, I have never heard him change his tune. How can that be? Does he not see what is in front of his face or does he lump us into the same category?

I have come to realize something else since the funeral. Dad will align himself with whomever he thinks can do the most for him. That person will be wonderful until they either neglect one of his needs or don't call when he wants to talk. Then on to the next one. It has taught me to watch my back in a way I never thought you should have to do with a parent. Was there ever any love or trust to begin with or was it all my mom's doing? I think if she wouldn't have been there, there would have been very little attention from this man for his children. She was able to control him in some way we cannot.

Chapter 10: Thomas and Kathryn
The Next Secret: The Affair

The minute Kathryn walked into the office, Thomas kept his eye on her. He liked the way she looked. She wore a lilac suit with a large lace collar and the platform shoes popular in this day. She was trim and her hair was permed in short waves. She answered his questions politely and sat primly in the interview chair. Thomas hired her on the spot. She would start Monday.

Thomas whistled on his way to work on Monday and walked in with a spring in his step. This really was ludicrous, he thought, the woman was married after all. But, still he could look.

Kathryn was nervous before work but dressed with care and knew that this position was a step up for her. Her boss, the man named Thomas was nice, she thought, and bright. This job could mean a better apartment and better food on the table, maybe even nylons. She would be careful to do things right.

Each night the office worked until 6 pm when dusk fell. Thomas would walk Kathryn to the bus stop and make sure she got safely off to home before going his separate way on another bus. It was too difficult to get a car even if you had the money. Most all industry was dedicated to the war effort now. On their brief walks, they got to know each other in a polite way. Thomas came to understand that Kathryn's husband worked the night shift in a local factory and she was often alone. She had married young and was the daughter of immigrants, a common story in this time and place. She never mentioned her husband and Thomas never brought him up either.

After about a month of these casual encounters, Thomas and his boss were sitting near Kathryn in the office one day talking about their craving for a home cooked meal. Kathryn overheard and openly asked them both to dinner, proudly telling them what a good cook she was. Thomas' eyes lit up. He and his boss would go to dinner that Friday evening. His boss's wife was in California so the timing was perfect. Some part of Kathryn thought it was an innocent and kind gesture to make to the two men. Another part of her was less sentimental and knew that this was a risk. This dinner could change her life forever.

Kathryn prepared carefully for the dinner. She told her husband what she would be doing while he would be working and he just shrugged. After his shift in the factory, he was too tired to care much about anything. On Friday, she left on her work clothes, carefully tied on an apron and set to work in her small apartment kitchen to prepare a roast chicken with potatoes. For dessert she would serve a cake, one of the things she made well from scratch. Dinner was successful and Thomas and his boss were relaxed and comfortable. Most of the talk centered on people or things at work and then after dessert, Thomas' boss said his goodbyes and went on his way. Thomas decided to stay and Kathryn let him.

Kathryn was almost mesmerized by Thomas. He was *so* different from her husband. Her husband had no fire, no goals, no zest. After working ten hours a night in the factory he was exhausted and their different schedules made no time for fun, love or excitement. Not that Kathryn had expected that when they were married. She was content to have escaped her parent's house, to have her own apartment and her own life. She wouldn't have missed other opportunities except one happened to show up on her doorstep. She enjoyed her work; she had a way with numbers, worked hard and took pride in it. Growing up, she had only two dresses that constantly had to be interchanged and so now being able to have several work outfits that were smart and stylish was a great achievement. She would analyze every clothing choice and enjoyed it so much.

The way Thomas looked at Kathryn made her feel beautiful and desirable. Her husband didn't have the energy to show her that look and maybe never did. Thomas was a college man and that made him a level above the people she knew. Her brothers didn't even get to finish high school, and Thomas seemed so intelligent. He grew up out of state although it was just across the river and to Kathryn that seemed as exotic as living in another country. Psychologists will tell you that the children of immigrants will work extra hard to try to fit in because they feel that they don't quite belong even though they were born here. They know how different their families are from other American families. They have different food, different customs and even a different language. Thomas' family had been in this country since the 1600s. His family was truly established here.

That night, after dinner, she told Thomas that her husband would not be home until near daybreak. That is the only mention she made of her husband. Thomas was quick to pick up on it. They had a glass of wine after dinner and lingered over the table after they were left alone. Gradually, Kathryn cleared away the dishes and cleaned up the kitchen with Thomas gallantly helping. They were somewhat polite and reserved at first and then gradually relaxed. Thomas told Kathryn about his background, his college days and what he thought about the war effort. Kathryn hung on his every word, afraid to interject too much for fear that Thomas wouldn't think she was intelligent enough. Thomas loved an audience just for him and he lapped it up.

As the evening grew later, Thomas felt encouraged and kissed Kathryn quickly and pausing only briefly, slowed it down until he found an answering response in her. She was stunned and also felt the stirrings of a longing she hadn't felt before.

That night she would lie in bed first with Thomas and then much later, after Thomas had left, hear her husband come in, shower and come to bed but she did not acknowledge him. He wouldn't expect her to, either.

Dear Mom,

I always noticed that when you were happy, Dad was unhappy, and vice versa. As I got older, and studied psychology, I realized that you seemed to be locked in a power struggle, which I learned was the first stage of marriage. I thought that after all those years you both had learned so little. How judgmental I was. It was so much deeper than something as trivial as a power struggle that makes it sound as if you both wanted to play with the same toy and one or the other of you had to win. It was more about the essence of you both, that there was a deep need to see the other bend. I know that part of what you felt was driven by the constant coldness you felt emanating from my father and since you had to live with it day after day, you had to make choices how to cope with it. You knew what he was capable of and what he was not.

You used to tell me that Grandma, Dad's mother, was cruel to you after my brothers were born. She wrote you a letter and told you that the twins' heads looked misshapen and that you needed to clean yourself up. You never forgave her and never really got over it. I used to wonder why you just didn't strike back, say something, stand up for yourself but instead you still went to visit her on our monthly visits to her home and were remote but polite. As a result, I never really knew Grandma because you instilled your distrust of her into me. At times I would resent that but now I am glad I was protected from her possible wrath. I thought perhaps Grandma was jealous. Once your daughter-in-law gives birth to your son's child you have truly lost the son perhaps? She saw you and the babies as threats to her son's attention to her. So…the question becomes where was my father in all this? Surely you told him about the letter, surely he knew how wounded you were but where the hell was he to defend you, tell you that you were still beautiful after giving birth to two babies, that you didn't have to be perfectly manicured after changing countless diapers (and they weren't disposables), sterilizing formula bottles and listening to endless crying all day. Surely, surely he let you know of his love?

Love, Your more sympathetic daughter

Chapter 11: Running For Cover

One of the things I remember most was my father's anger. We would never want to provoke him because no good would come of it. I never saw him physically hurt my mother and I don't think he ever did, but there are worse wounds, wounds of the heart. I remember once that a neighbor behind us grew tomatoes and a little boy talked me into picking a few of them through the chain link fence that divided their yard from ours. I was only about five years old. Stupidly, I put the tomatoes in the garage to play a game with later. The neighbor saw what I did and told my father. The neighbor had plentiful tomato plants and certainly didn't need the ones I took, but they were "old school" and had no children to begin with. They weren't going to forgive me one transgression. So my father yelled at me for what I did and sent me to bed right after dinner during the summer when the sun still shone late into the evening. He made me go to bed every night like that for two weeks and refused to speak to me or pay attention to me any other time. Finally, my mother suggested that I apologize to my father, which I did, and was let off the hook. It wasn't so much what I did as that I made my father look bad and "let him down" thus starting a cycle to try to receive his love and attention which had me dangling like a puppet on a string. I would bring home straight "A's" from school and receive no pat on the back because it was expected of me. Then he told me that college was needless for a woman *but* I would probably get a better grade of husband if I attended. In his later years, he would deny ever saying that for times have changed so drastically. It wouldn't be politically correct anymore to even think it and he wouldn't want to "look bad."

Another time, when I was about five, my mother was busy cleaning up my room and really threatening to throw all my treasures away because she had totally lost her patience with the disorganization. I was sobbing and crying when my father got home from work. My father asked why I was crying and when my mother told him she was throwing away some of my things he screamed at her to put my stuff away and get me to shut up. She ran sobbing into the basement and I remember tiptoeing down the stairs to see her sitting in the dark, drinking a beer, something she rarely did. I tried to climb into her lap but she rejected me at first and I felt so awful for her because I understood too well what it meant to have my father angry. My sympathy for her was overwhelming and I felt enormous guilt for being the cause of this. That started me trying to save her. I never could.

Going to McDonalds with my dad one day made me aware that you didn't anger him. We were at the original style McDonalds with the arches where you stood outside to order. The kid working behind the counter, was trying to remember the order for hamburgers and milkshakes, they didn't have a lot of options back then. They used a paper and pencil to write it on an order pad and for some reason this boy wouldn't write it down and every time he called the order to the back he got it wrong. Finally, my father had had enough and yelled (in front of everyone) that he should "write the Goddamn order down right." I wanted to shrink into the background. It didn't take much to realize that everyone was staring and seeing someone get so angry was sobering.

Any time my father went out in public, be it a grocery store, restaurant, whatever, you would immediately feel the hair raise on the back of your neck at certain signs from my father. If he was ready to blow, you would first see a stiff mouth emerge and then a hard look in his eyes, then he would shake his head and move his arm as though he was going to pound the table and then you better clear the area. I guess the irony of all this was that my father was not a large man like his own father; he was more like the runt of the litter. Even his sister was taller than him. So what made him think he could treat people like this? Was it in his genes?

My brothers were often fighting between themselves. They say most twins are unusually close but my brothers had to beat the statistics and be extremely competitive. My father came upon them fighting when they were supposed to be raking leaves and one of them received a rake in the side of the face. The offending one was marched off to the basement and my dad leaned him over the sawhorse and whipped him with a belt. I could never forgive my father for that, for his lack of self-control and his corporeal punishment. What was even worse was the way it totally cowed my brother. He was subdued for days, like his very soul had been stripped from him. I was appalled and also afraid. I never understood how my mother let it happen. But then, I don't know what I expected her to do.

My father was called to jury duty more than once while I was growing up. It was very interesting to hear my father's view on the cases. One involved a paternity suit where the woman explained how the baby in question was conceived. Supposedly, she and the baby's father were in a car and had sex. When it came out in the trial that the car was parked under a streetlight my father said he knew right then and there that the woman was lying. No one would have sex under a streetlight! I wondered if my father had ever in his entire life known passion and love and a longing so intense that nothing else would matter. It was inconceivable to him.

The facts as known:

My parents always told me that they had met at work. Since my mother refused to ever speak of her first marriage, only briefly, to explain that the man had married her on the rebound and that she left him because he didn't want children.

We found out about her marriage from a genealogy book at my grandmother's house. It had her name listed differently than her maiden or married name which, of course, incited questions. I remember very clearly that she became firm and said we would discuss it when we got home. Once home, she explained her self-concocted story about the man and that was that. I once brought up a question about her first marriage, being naturally curious and still very young. She lashed out at me and told me to never ever speak of it again. I was so shocked by her reaction that I thought divorce must be the ugliest things to ever happen in one's life.

After her death, my father just started talking and couldn't seem to stop. For the two weeks after her death, he would tell me the details of his first meeting with my mother and told me, with a little bit of shining pride in his eyes, that he had dinner with her at her place and he didn't go home afterwards. He seemed rather proud of that, cuckolding another man's wife.

My father's sudden openness about the affair was quite a surprise. It was almost as if there were my mother's shadowy hand at his back, pushing him forward to speak, as though a reluctant child being brought forward to stand on stage for the first time. My mother did promise to tell me things, she just didn't happen to stay around long enough to do it. Perhaps, this was her way of accomplishing it.

Chapter 12: Transition

After I found out the prognosis on my mother, I decided to fly up to see her and assess the situation. Having a sister-in-law who was a nurse helped me know what signs to look for that the cancer was progressing. What I found was a huge frustration.

My mother had been told by the cancer specialist that she could have an operation that would help against future pain but not cure her. Her cancer had already spread to her liver and that would kill her. However, the doctor refused to put a timeline on the progression of the disease and implied it could be up to two years before the end. Since I heard about the x-rays and I researched the Internet thoroughly, I knew it would be only a matter of months. I was hoping for at least six months but the Internet said probably three. When I saw her, it was obviously progressing at a fast pace. With only three weeks from the first symptom, she already showed signs of swelling, shortness of breath and fatigue. Worse was seeing that she was teaching my father how to do laundry and she was not cleaning his bathroom (she could never look at dirt and let it be). I cleaned what I could without insulting her and encouraged good nutrition and other things. Unfortunately, she was in total denial about the eventual outcome and wouldn't discuss such mundane things as her wishes for the approaching end. My father had been having crying jags for the last three weeks and he would just dissolve into tears at any time, so totally out of character.

My mother stood by me as I cleaned my dad's bathroom and handed me the mop. "You know your father is crying for himself, not for me," she said emphatically. She told me that the only thing he had said to her since the diagnosis was that she had been a joy in his life. No declarations of love, no sentiments, no nothing. She was bitter about it and told me not to let him take the money intended for the grandchildren when she passes. At the time, I saw her as being unforgiving and too one sided. I knew I couldn't stop the outcome of her disease and I longed to open up and pour out my heart but she wasn't open to it. When someone is dying, you have to do things their way.

I returned in two weeks with my children and we spent a good weekend altogether with my brothers, their family and even knew laughter. Her symptoms were much worse, her eating had slacked off and I knew it was an effort for her now to do everyday things. She tried to make it so normal for my children and I truly knew how much that took out of her. She was wonderful, telling me her life was complete, she felt loved and that she had a wonderful family. I did notice that she never specifically mentioned my dad's name in her list of the people she loved.

Two significant things occurred. One was telling me she felt so loved because that had been a recurring theme in my life, trying to let her know she WAS loved and hoping it would make a difference. The other was the way she looked me directly in the eyes and said sincerely, "Thank you" when I offered her a bag of adult diapers I knew she was in need of. My father had felt uncomfortable just going out and buying them. She had always had trouble saying thank you to us. That simple phrase raised the hair on the back of my neck. If she was saying this, then it was the end.

I was able to hug her over and over and tell her I loved her and she told me she loved me back. All pretenses and veils were brushed aside and only the truth showed through. I will forever be grateful for this opportunity and my children have carried on with their lives knowing they completed their cycle with her, by laying their heads on her shoulder, hugging her and telling her all their memories of their times with her and of their love for her.

A week later, she was taken to the hospice. My father had been having difficulty getting her up to the bathroom and she had been sleeping more and more. He called the hospice that took her away in an ambulance, alone. My father stayed home, took a shower and ate lunch while his wife of 58 years was taken away from her home for the last time, set up in a strange room and started her countdown to the end of her life. He had done all this without telling any of us children. The relief in his voice when he did talk to me was somewhat chilling. I thought that perhaps the stress of the situation had pushed him a bit over the edge.

It took only four days for the end to come. I was arranging care for my children and was back at home, out of state, and had gotten my husband's sister to fly down to stay with my kids. We were in a restaurant the evening before I was to return to my mother and I thought I heard my cell phone ring. I looked at my watch and it was 6:10 pm. I started to pick up my cell phone but it wasn't ringing and at that point and I thought I could not take the kind of call I was afraid it would be, in a restaurant, in front of the children. We paid the check and went home. There was a message on my answering machine at home. My mother had passed away at 6:10 but my brother had not called my cell phone, only the home phone. Eerie.

My brothers had both been at her side at the end, stroking her hair, holding her hand and telling her they loved her and that it was okay to go on. When she passed less than a minute after my brother told her it was okay, my father who had been standing back away from the end of the bed, ran into the bathroom and threw up. Afterwards, my brother's wife urged my father to stay in the room and say his goodbyes. He pleaded with them not to make him. They nudged him into the room and shut the door. Later, he would say that he didn't want to do that, he was forced to go and that he didn't even know what closure meant. He just didn't want to be in a room with a dead person, even his wife.

I sat in the funeral home with one of my brothers and my dad, making the arrangements. At times, my father was rude to the funeral home director, making sly remarks about the cost and what they provided. He didn't want any fuss. My brother stood up to him and told him this was about what Mom wanted, not him and we were doing things the way she wanted. My dad backed down. He was outnumbered.

Chapter 13: From The Other Side

Almost thirty years ago, I attended a funeral for the mother of a friend. The mother had been brutally murdered on New Year's Day. At the funeral, attended by almost two hundred people, I remember vividly that my friend got up and in a clear voice told about what she would miss not having a mother. My throat constricted so tightly I could barely breathe, and I will never, never forget the things she said. She would never again have the joy of giving her mom a present, never see her smile as she opened it, never see her give her granddaughter a hug nor see her do all the little day-to-day things that you take for granted. It wasn't the things that had happened that she would remember as much as the things that she had been robbed of, that she would miss. Every waking moment would hold the knowledge that her mother was no longer there. Every possibility in her life had changed. Nothing would ever be the same or as it was supposed to be. Her daughter would now grow up without a grandmother, she would never again be able to obtain advice, unburden herself to her mom, or exchange a recipe. Life was forever and absolutely changed.

Partly because of this experience I knew to leave no unfinished business with my mother. I was also aware that my mother was an "older" mom. That meant I wouldn't have her with me during the last half of my life and so, especially in the last few years, I tried never to let a week go by without some kind of contact with her even though several states separated us. During her last weeks on earth, I felt compelled to help my mother in any way possible and took it upon myself personally to help ease her pain, both physically and spiritually. However, you can't help anyone until they ask for it, so just letting her know I was there was the most I could do for several weeks.

Until my last visit, when we were able to tell her how much we loved her and she was able to receive it. I felt unsettled, trying to figure out how to let all this end in the best possible way. In the end, it wasn't for me to decide what she needed but it was entirely up to her, it was her life script, not mine.

I have been exploring life and death, the afterlife and spirituality almost my entire life. I believe that part of my quest has been motivated by the need to look elsewhere in my life for happiness. When I wasn't happy at home or feeling appreciated it never made sense to me that life would only be this. God wouldn't be so unfair, would he? So, I looked elsewhere and played with ways to find the answers to my questions outside of the normal means. I visited psychics, mediums and intuitives from time to time who can read "energy" and tell me what they see. It's like going to a psychologist, but one who cuts through all the crap and tells you like it is. You just have to remember that the quality of the session depends on just how clearly the intuitive reads you and whether or not they are filtering it through their own experiences. Then, you have to make a choice of whether you want that reality to happen or use free will and change it if you can. Some things you can't change, and some you can change a little bit, and some things never happen. This has been a great source of comfort to me because it is like a confirmation of my intuition. Sometimes, you get just a little information and sometimes you get a lot. There is nothing like a very good intuitive for getting you in touch with reality and giving you a kick in the pants.

Today, I went to see a healer that uses energy and intuition as well as oriental medicine. As she began to test for health problems she felt a presence in the room and mentally asked who it was. It was you, Mom, and the message you wanted to tell us was that when you were still here, you really appreciated my kids visiting you and the memories you all enjoyed. The healer said that this was a special moment and one the kids would remember all their lives. I will also remember. It will be one of the moments that made me know with certainty what lovely human beings my kids were becoming, for their love for you shone so strongly with no thought of how you looked or what would come, but they just stayed in the moment with you and your love. Your response of love was so sincere and so strong that they are lucky to have that to always think about as they grow older. You were the one person in their life who showed them unconditional love and I thank you so much for that, Mom. You were always there for them, thinking about them, sending them letters and little tidbits of love.

The healer said that your energy was strong, vibrant and rested. It was a positive energy, the one I always knew was inside you. So now, your spirit knows things that I can only guess, you can see everything clearly with no veil separating you from the truth. What bliss that must be.

I miss my mother, miss her in many ways but I also am happy for her. She is true to her form now, free in spirit with "her scarf blowing in the wind" and back to her original form, before she came into a physical world and "forgot" her true identity. That is what we all do and some of us still remember and long to be in spirit form again. Others of us seem to lap up the physical world easily and enjoy all its gifts. It all depends on those lessons you have taken on to learn this time around in the physical form.

I've read about soul groups before, the theory that you incarnate over and over with the same group of souls playing out different parts and each time learning a different lesson. I think that at one time my mother was a sister to me for that just feels right. I often wonder how a soul that is not related to me in this incarnation physically, can feel like someone I know so well, and someone I am related to physically can feel so alien. I guess different souls come in and out depending on the lessons needed.

I know that my mother and one of my brothers have been together for eons. There is a soul closeness there that will live forever. I know I will see my mother again but I wonder if you ever get over the roles that we have all played until we come back to earth again and again forgetting our "spirit" selves. When I pass over, will I see her on the other side and go running to her, yelling, "Mom!"

Chapter 14: That's Life

My own life lesson involves trying to stop taking care of everyone else instead of myself. How did I finally end up knowing this and why didn't I own it sooner? Well, thinking back to my childhood and knowing that the families we were born into help us to learn these lessons, I can see that my father was emotionally distant so I tried to please people to get the approval I couldn't get from him. My mother never gave me her approval either because she was to shaken up with all her own issues to realize what she was doing. She didn't want me to get a "big head;" conceit was one of the worst offenses. But some of us needed to be pumped up a bit and some of us felt it more acutely than others.

From the time I was little, I started trying to please my parents and kept right on going trying to please my teachers and anyone else in a position of authority. Even in high school, I tried to please my boyfriends which often involved keeping my opinions to myself and not letting them see any strength. Even if they didn't see it, I hope they felt it anyway.

My husband asked me if I was depressed over the recent holidays. I said no and asked why, puzzled. He said because it was the first holiday without my mother. Ahhh! It didn't seem to bother me then. I can't tell you why. But today is a different story. Today is my birthday and I acutely feel the loss. I guess because Mom would always remember and it was always a big deal.

My brothers and I were born in January and when we were little my mother couldn't afford to buy much and knew we would be overwhelmed with it anyway so close to Christmas, so she started celebrating our "half birthday" in July. We would have a cake and a few presents then, just like a real birthday. All my friends were intensely jealous and it was one of the few times I did feel special. The thoughtfulness of my mother lives on in what she did with that. So...I guess birthdays are one of the few times when I felt taken care of. I didn't have to do anything for anyone else and I could accept with good grace that someone would want to make my day special.

But today...the children have gone their separate ways to their activities, my husband is out of town, and there was only one card in the mail, from a distant friend, not even a relative. I know my father has sent a card, just not in time, and my in-laws will realize the day eventually. It's just not the same, to know that there was one person in the entire world, one person who shared the same day because she was the one giving birth, that knows the importance of this day to me, and she is gone. I am as close to tears today as I have ever been since her passing. And I try not to think selfishly about this. She is in a better place and it was her time to go but I wish I could see her face one more time.

There is something special about a mother's love, even with its flaws. There is only this one person that carried us so closely, actually inside their bodies. We knew their heartbeats and their emotions and I think that is fused within our cells so that when they are gone, it's truly as if a part of us has been left behind, a part of us has stopped beating.

My son has said often times that he doesn't really want to grow up because he knows that at some point I will die. I try to tell him that it is a part of life, that I want him to live his life un-emcumbered by guilt about what will happen to me. I want him to realize every dream in his heart, every urge in his soul and live his life fully. My greatest sacrifice is telling him this because inside I do wish to cling to him forever. But that is not right. A mother must be strong for her child. And one day, when he reaches the age that proclaims him an adult, perhaps he will not care so much anymore. That is nature's way of letting children separate from their parents. They start to think more and more and about themselves and less so about their parents and that relationship. So, I will let him pull away from me as nature has intended and remember to leave no unfinished business with him and my other son. I will always let them know love and warmth and that I am so grateful they chose to be born to me. I will back away slowly as they show their need for more space and distance. I will go into the background where I will wait patiently for them to need me once more.

Dear Mom,

Thank you for the things you did that made certain events in my childhood unique. Do you remember those once a year trips to the amusement park where there was a muddy swimming hole and rides that threw you upside down? I know you didn't enjoy going. Our excitement just propelled you along. We would ride all those rides and you would pack a picnic lunch. You would walk patiently around while we amused ourselves, never riding any of the rides yourself, or doing any of the games. We used to swim, too, until you realized how unsanitary the water was and put your foot down about that.

I used to love to buy you presents because you never bought much for yourself. I would save my allowance and then make Dad take me up to the store or else walk up to the nearby department store and look around. There was one dress I can see you wearing because it was blue checked and had a double ruffle around the scooped neckline and the waist had a fabric belt. I thought you looked so beautiful in it. I imagine you wore it so as not to hurt my feelings and am not sure if you would have bought it for yourself. You wore it to the amusement park that one summer. I still see you vividly. Your hair was still brown and curly and your eyes matched the vivid blue of the dress. You still had that twinkle in your eyes then.

Back when I was about five years old, I used to act like I was running away and then would come back as a different person, knocking on the front door like a visitor. My brothers would be howling with laughter, and to your credit, you never once made fun of me or made me feel stupid, but went along with my game. I often did this at dinnertime. I can't imagine how frustrating it was for you to be in the kitchen cooking dinner for an ungrateful family and have to take the time out to answer the door and pretend I was someone else and show me around. You were such a good sport about that. I love you for letting me pretend. I love you for not letting my brothers make fun of it.

When I was about nine years old, the Beatles were at their heyday. My girlfriend and I would put on tights and our father's baggy, button-down oxford cloth shirts and dance around the house listening to the music, turned up high. We thought we were so cool and you let us be, let us go on until you must have wanted to scream but you never did. We also went through a giggling phase where we could laugh for an hour at absolutely nothing. How annoying we must have been. Thank you for putting up with that.

But then, Mom, what happened? Something in the house changed when I was nine or ten years old. Some decision was not made or some event that was supposed to happen, didn't. It was as if a candle was snuffed out, a light turned dark. I knew something had changed but I didn't know what and still don't. It was if the light in you was being extinguished and there was no joy in your heart. I thought for a long time that perhaps because I was getting older, that maybe you didn't enjoy me anymore. My brothers had already become teenagers and were definitely more difficult. You told me once that you loved small children the most. A classmate of mine and her mother were at the same store that we walked into. The other mother was helping my classmate pick out new clothes and remarked on how much she loved being part of her daughter's life now that she was older, picking out trendy clothes, looking at hairstyles, considering the lightest of makeup. You were so emphatic afterwards, telling me that she was so wrong that it was when the children were young, that a mother's heart was the fullest. I was so hurt, and because of the look in your eye, could not tell you that the thought you expressed had deeply wounded me. You didn't even notice my hurt.

Love, Your daughter, still wondering

Chapter 15: Moving On

Kathryn sat at her kitchen table, alone, pondering what had happened in her life. She had started seeing Thomas on a regular basis, sneaking him inside her apartment, meeting him elsewhere and it was tearing her apart inside. What was she doing? Thomas was everything that her husband was not, authoritative, confident, outgoing. She felt different around Thomas, like there were endless possibilities for her life and an immense freedom. With her husband, she felt that there were years of drudgery ahead with no end. She would work and work and eventually wither away and her husband would just be one more factory "Joe." With Thomas, she could have a little house with a few kids and live the American dream. Although a first generation American, she still had one foot in Eastern Europe and couldn't run away from the fact that her family still spoke their native tongue when together.

Kathryn and Thomas were in her apartment one day and her mother came over. She rushed to have Thomas hide in the small bathroom and told her mother that she was ill and just couldn't see her. This produced tons of guilt for her to deal with and tore her heart apart even more. Thomas was now professing his love and it was like a dizzying, forbidden fruit that was too sweet to resist. She gloried in being in love while she was wrenched in half about what she was doing to her husband, who was becoming almost nonexistent to her.

She knew the turmoil had to end and finally found the courage to ask a friend for advice. Her friend knew a lawyer that could help her but in those days you had to prove just cause for a divorce. She met with the lawyer and to her surprise she easily made up a story about her husband not wanting children and thus found a reason for the divorce. The lawyer felt she had a case and would help her. When she finally told her husband, it was very difficult for her. She didn't want to hurt him and he was stunned but also knew that they were no longer on the same wavelength. She was relieved and was able to turn her full attention now to Thomas. She moved out of her apartment and in with a girlfriend. It was a taste of freedom, being more on her own than she had ever been. Before, everyone had always told her what to do and this was fun.

Kathryn was now able to see Thomas more openly and the people at work began to glance at them with knowing and all seeing eyes. They didn't care. Kathryn now gave into her feelings of being helplessly in love and positively glowed with it. Thomas grew more demanding of Kathryn's time and her physical love. She felt wanted and needed and gave herself freely. She felt truly and absolutely in love.

The Scene

As she walked into the packed hearing room, she could feel the eyes of the men, and also the women, boring into her back. The women tittered as they leaned next to their companions and whispered the rumors. The men looked at her appreciatively and almost smacked their lips. She was tempted to sway her hips a bit to inflame the situation, but instead she squared her shoulders and stood up straighter.

She had to pass several of the committee members on her way to the witness chair. They eyed her in a different way, trying to determine her role in all this, to assess just who she really was. It was rather unnerving to her normal confidence.

She had to pass by *him* too. She glanced over in the most perfunctory way, hoping to not make any eye contact. Seeing him there and knowing she was about to support his unraveling gave her a twinge, that is, until he winked at her. She almost gasped aloud and then, with renewed determination, took her seat on the witness stand.

Chapter 16: Personalities

After the divorce from her husband, Kathryn found out more about Thomas' relationship with Lydia, his girlfriend from college. One evening, Thomas and Kathryn went to a movie and a woman was there with a group of other women. The woman ran up to Thomas, before seeing Kathryn, and gave him a hug and a kiss, positively beaming at him. Thomas was uncomfortable and stiff lipped. He didn't hug her back and as the woman drew away it was then she noticed Kathryn standing there with an odd look on her face. Thomas introduced Kathryn to Lydia and Lydia studied Kathryn and then looked questioningly at Thomas. It was obvious that Lydia was deeply puzzled and disturbed. Thomas refused to explain the situation. With one last hurtful look at Thomas, Lydia ran from the theater and Thomas pulled Kathryn ahead to find a seat. Kathryn was still stunned about the affectionate display and looked at Thomas searchingly. Thomas told her that it was a woman he used to date. Kathryn accepted the answer at face value and would come to rationalize it to mean that she was lucky to have won a sought after man. It wouldn't be until years later that the truth would come out and Kathryn would find out that Lydia had also thought that she and Thomas were a couple, almost engaged. Thomas had been seeing Lydia at the same time he had started seeing Kathryn. Lydia had even moved from another city to be with him, thinking that marriage was imminent. Thomas and Lydia went back to his college days of moonlight dances and the orchestra sounds of swing.

He had been attracted to Lydia's panache, but Kathryn would win him in the end because of her sweetness and sincerity and perhaps also because of her willingness to go along with whatever he said.

Kathryn was jealous and also felt foolish for assuming that Thomas was entirely trustworthy. She had done the unthinkable, had an affair and gotten a divorce, a terribly scandalous thing to do and all because of Thomas. But Thomas continued to woo her, continued to see her and he chose her. So Kathryn put aside her feelings of doubt and married Thomas although the jealous feelings were to rear their ugly head many times during her marriage.

Thomas got drafted into the army and did training in different cities. He was lucky never to fight in the war or go overseas. He trained in Mississippi and was then stationed back in Dayton, Ohio. His sister, Mid, was working at the base since before the war. She happened to work for a two star general. Thomas' transfer was supposedly because the base was understaffed and needed more recruits.

Kathryn was relieved that Thomas was able to stay in the States. Her brothers were busy fighting in Europe. One ended up with malaria and almost died. Everyone was grateful just to be alive. The war created shortages of all things made out of metal. As the war wound down, limited consumer items became available. It was incredible to be able to buy a refrigerator and be put on the lottery list to buy a car. Thomas and Kathryn were one of the chosen ones when their offer to buy a car was accepted. Absolutely everyone needed a car and was trying to purchase one. As soon as they received it, offers came in from others to buy it at a profit to Thomas and Kathryn. However, transportation was too valuable and they kept it.

The war also made day-to-day squabbles and unhappiness seem trivial. All over, people lost their loved ones. To not have lost a father, a brother, or a husband was a great and wonderful gift. So any problems being experienced by the newly married couple were put into the background. People were just too glad to be alive, to have a roof over their heads and food on the table.

Those unresolved problems may one day come back to haunt them, but not now. Now was about survival.

Thomas was grateful to his sister and whoever had a hand in helping him with the transfer. She and her husband lived nearby Kathryn and Thomas. Mid, having decided to absolutely never bring children into this world, was slim and trim and elegant, she hadn't been a "most beautiful" for no reason. Her black hair was thick and shiny and much of her income was spent on clothing. She was an excellent cook and liked to entertain. She had an unforgiving and hard edge to her, however. She was rather outspoken about her opinions, this was not a woman that you would describe as warm. She could be charming but she was not loving.

Kathryn began to long for children. However, the wartime economy was still a concern and a family would have to wait. She was constantly put in a situation where she was with Mid. She often felt that Mid looked down her nose at her. Kathryn's "immigrant" status was a strike against her. Mid was opinionated and those opinions would often hurt Kathryn's feelings. Mid might make a comment about certain shoes being so ugly and then realize Kathryn owned a pair. She might comment on certain dishes being so common and then notice that Kathryn served them for dinner. Nothing Mid did was overt, but was subtle, like a slow growing cancer. Kathryn, knowing how much Mid had done for Thomas, choked down her resentment and carried on. Kathryn tried hard to get along, but sometimes she would almost cry in despair of ever living up to Mid's standards.

Strangely, it was James who showed his approval of Kathryn as a mate for Thomas. James was in the last decade of his life when Thomas married and Thomas and Kathryn would drive the two hours to visit James and Anna regularly. James' shrewd intelligence was a good match for Kathryn's intellect. They both liked to play board games and Kathryn earned James' respect by often winning. She was subservient enough not to be a threat to his ego but still spunky enough to make James enjoy her company.

Anna saw Kathryn as a rival. She, of course, acted like she accepted Kathryn, and as long as they visited regularly kept her talons sheathed. Occasionally, Kathryn would feel the barbs Anna shot her way, but Kathryn understood that she had taken something from Anna, meaning Thomas, and was content to be a target. Overall, she accepted the situation of Thomas' family and their intricate web of animosity and egos. Kathryn was always careful to not offend and to be immaculately dressed. Anna could be very particular in her standards.

Chapter 17: A Man's World

It must be for some good reason that I am surrounded by men. Growing up I had two brothers. Now I have two sons. My mother is gone and that leaves me with a father, still two brothers, a husband and two sons. When I was young, I lived in the era that has taken thirty years to ebb, an era where little girls had some very definitive rolls to play. I had to wear dresses to school and that dress code didn't change until I was in high school. I rebelled so heartily that I ended up wearing blue jeans, flannel shirts and hiking boots. Ah, but I didn't forget my make up. Arggghhh!

I didn't like the roles a lot of my female classmates played because, even if they were smart, they often just thought about boys and how to manipulate them into asking them out. The worst part was that my parents had a very strict interpretation of what a "lady" should be. A lady shouldn't run (this meant no sports), a lady should be proper in her language (double standards for boys and girls), girls get married to someone who can take care of them (girls are too dumb to stand on their own), and girls don't matter as much as boys.

I grew up valuing logic. I wanted to be a man because a man got to realize their dreams of a career and to be anything he wanted to be. Girls were second-class citizens. I came to a point where I never cried in front of my family, never showed emotion. I wonder why no one thought this odd. For now, I look back at that tortured girl and see that she was just struggling to survive, feeling lost and abandoned. Where was her mother, who was supposed to protect her? Her mother was lost in a web of her own making, of guilt and loss. But, out of pain often comes strength and when I look back I also see a girl learning that pain can make you strong. I became a rebel, fighting against society's standards. Whereas, back then I spoke boldly and often out of turn, I learned to wield diplomacy and try to achieve a win-win situation, instead of trying to win a battle. People know they can't mess with my integrity, they know I'll fight a wrong, but do it in such a way that everyone can walk away with no regrets. I hope they see the power in this, in me. I *have finally* found my power.

Dear Mom,

I used to think that if you loved someone enough, you should be able to overcome all obstacles, even mental illness. I reasoned that if you loved enough, you would put their welfare above your own and do what had to be done to protect them and keep them happy. It's not quite so cut and dried. Now that I know the secret of the affair and the guilt you must have carried, I know your version of what it took to protect us and my version are entirely different. In your day, divorce was a scandal and so how could you, an immigrant's daughter, struggling with all sorts of disadvantages, think you could possibly buck the system and be divorced twice? You would never have acknowledged that could even be done, so you had to make the best of what you must have presumed to be a trap. My father was only as sensitive to you in relationship to how much of his needs were fulfilled. If you scratched his back, you might get a little in return. If not, you would be ignored. I still remember some of the strange ideas you would get, trying to rationalize away any illnesses or pains by thinking that it was the odor of the new detergent or that your swelling from the cancer must be due to tomato juice or the vitamin you choked down. Those odd ideas made an effective wall around you. No one could talk to you and convince you otherwise. You went for years with skin so dry your arms would peel and you gained weight too easily, classic symptoms of thyroid deficiency and it took absolute insistence from the rest of us for you to finally see a doctor and get a prescription and the symptoms disappeared. Once, you had an eyelid infection that swelled your eyelid and it was like that for an entire year. Dad said you looked like a drunk and he finally yelled something distasteful and you went to the doctor. Again, the prescription made the problem disappear within days. All those weeks of not doing anything when it could have been gone almost overnight. I wondered if your mistrust of help had anything to do with reality or if you did those things to distance yourself deliberately. I began to see you more and more as a wounded animal and I tried so hard to get through to you. I imagined that your first husband must have abused you and that you had never fully recovered. I thought such terrible things and ached for you. But then, things would happen that made me dislike you.

You acted jealous of me at times, but no, that can't be right, mothers don't do that. Once, while still in high school, a national magazine was looking for regional "reporters" to feed them information, I applied and wrote an article and was accepted. When I proudly told you, you turned away telling me that the magazine, that you had *never* read, "was going downhill in recent years." Another time, you told me that you would finally give me my special centennial piano once I married. Since I wasn't married until later in my twenties, I asked for the piano and you said no. Then you gave it to my niece and moved it to her house before I even got to comment. At times, when I would dress up to go out on a date, you would make disparaging comments about the way I looked, telling me that I could do better. You didn't want me putting on airs. Being confident was a mortal sin to you.

The most painful thing was when I suffered several miscarriages and you actually thought I was making them up.

You said that miscarriages weren't real and that they just couldn't happen. I tried so hard to ignore the pain you caused me. But even now, after all that has gone on, after all the secrets I have learned, it still hurts to have felt so alone. I know the lesson I was learning was that I am enough. I don't need anyone else to validate me or tell me I am okay. But what a tough lesson to learn from the bosom of my mother.

Love, Your still resentful daughter (after all)

Chapter 18: Crocodile Tears

My father continued to cry daily after the funeral. He would wake up in the morning and start to cry around breakfast time. He would sit at the counter stool in the kitchen with a dry piece of muffin or bagel and chew rhythmically, not looking left or right. He had always had this affliction that made his jaw click loudly every time he chewed, although it caused him no other troubles. His jaw clicked, his mouth worked and then he would start to cry and still try to chew his food and swallow. I was afraid that he would choke and I would have to do the Heimlich maneuver. I came to dread the mornings and would try to sleep in a bit to avoid the same breakfast hour. He was too crafty; he would get up early if he needed to, but still wait upon his breakfast until I was up, too. I lost five pounds in two weeks this way. Really.

He would cry. I would wait. I would try and comfort him. I would try and help him, explain to him the process of grief. Did he want to read about the process? No. Did he want to join a grief group? No, no. Did he want to talk to a professional? No. See the doctor? No. He kept moaning out during these episodes, "She was so beautiful." He explained that he kept seeing her on her deathbed and that vision was scarred onto his brain. He thought she looked so awful, and then he would compare her to when he met her and she was young and still glowing from youth and life, and the image would wrench him. The shallowness of that did not elude me.

He never came close to her bed as she died, he never held her hand. As she lost the strength to even talk, he scolded her and told her that they had to hear what she needed. My brothers, bless them, held her hands and stroked her hair and talked to her as though she were a baby, holding her while she breathed her last breath. So why did my father find her so repulsive? I think it was because his love was not based on who she was but on what she could do for him. Since she was no longer functional, then she was no longer desirable. How repugnant that was.

This cycle continued for the two weeks I spent with him. I got him a prescription to relax him and he would sleep quite a bit for a few days. The problem continued and he was so ashamed to be crying because men just don't do that kind of thing. He felt he would get over it soon, his marriage of fifty-eight years. He said that no one he knew ever showed their tears to anyone and that it just shouldn't last so long. After all, she had been dead two weeks, it was time to get on with things.

The day after the funeral he put me to work cleaning out every personal thing she owned. I shipped large boxes to my home and my brothers picked through sentimental items, choosing what they wanted to remember her by. My father kept nothing of her to remember. He wanted her presence cleansed from the house. I didn't question him. I did what he wanted and secretly thought he was a hateful person, but he was still my father. Perhaps part of me didn't want him to have anything of hers because he wouldn't appreciate it anyway. It would be like soiling it.

My father began to increasingly talk about when he was young or when he was still employed. He would tell long stories about all his memories, keeping the focus on himself. During all this, he never once asked how anybody else was coping, how anyone else was getting along with their own grief, how anyone else felt or what was happening in their life. I began to increasingly see that everything that had ever happened for us or been given to us was more a result of my mother than my father. He had upheld the illusion that he was doing these things, also, and my mother didn't dispel it. I think that was her real gift to us, the illusion that my father was there for us.

Chapter 19: Spirits Speak

I met a fascinating woman yesterday, a medium. I wanted to see if she could contact my mother and actually speak with her. She quietly explained her process on contacting the spirits and that everything is made up of energy so that using energy is all she really does, which technically is true, however gifts like hers are not a dime a dozen.

After her introduction, she explained that the spirits that choose to show up might not necessarily be persons that I liked in life. I thought this was kind of funny, like deciding to have a truce. But right away a spirit came in and it was someone I never thought would show up. It was Anna, my grandmother. I was never close to her and always wary of her tongue. I never knew if she would have a hidden barb behind the meaning of what she said. So.. I just stayed quiet a lot of the time. It was always evident that she idealized my dad and the rest of us just came along for the ride.

Anna started out by saying that she regrets not laughing more in life, that she was stoic and particular, that she considered her life happy but with lots of hard work. She described her death and where it occurred (validating that it really was her we were talking to) and then went on to say some things about her relationship with my grandfather. She told me (as I asked questions) that a widow with a child had certain financial needs and that my grandfather held the answer to those needs. He was available and could provide for her. I wondered how she could marry the man who had killed her husband and she said she was able to have blinders on and ignore the truth because otherwise she would not have been able to live with him or herself. Anna was also able to think of Bernie as her "other son" and Thomas became her "only son." I'm not sure how this kind of logic exists but I believe it. She described James as vindictive, hateful, punishing, cruel and with fits of temper. It was chilling to think that a man like that even had a wife, a son, a daughter. Shouldn't there be some way to keep people like that from bearing offspring? James never had remorse about the killing. Never.

After Anna left, my mother came in. I was bound and determined not to cry but the emotion welled up in my chest and I felt such longing to be with her. She laughed and asked if the noises she was making in my house startled me and I said that as long as I knew they were hers, I was fine with it. There had been banging going on in my house at times, which only started happening since my mother passed over. Things like the sliding glass doors making banging sounds when there was no wind. It's nice to have proof of her presence. She also told me that she was touched by the care I took in picking out what she would wear at the funeral. I was surprised at that because I just felt her body should be comfortable because comfort in clothing meant a lot to her when she was alive. She told me about my children and their quest in life, she told me about my own quest. I think I could have listened to her messages for an entire day. It was so comforting and loving. It was indeed an incredible gift and not one the general population experiences.

The medium explained her concept of energy and because we are all made of energy, every thought, everything we see, everything we feel is *all* energy. Energy works like radio waves and comes in different patterns and vibrations. We, as humans, can choose to vibrate at different levels, thus someone with negative intent may vibrate at a lower level and someone with a pure, loving intent may vibrate at a higher level. It is not a judgment on anyone, just the way it is. Once this is understood than there are choices to make. Choices involve the treatment of others as well as yourself. You can walk the high road or you can walk the low road.

Speaking to a lost loved one should be the most natural thing in the world. Most religions talk of an everlasting life, but Holy Moly, those spirits better not come and scare the bejeebies out of anyone. They teach that it is the dark side that comes through, but that makes no sense whatsoever. Losing a loved one is a loss but also a time to know they are really at peace. They are free of their human body and have no boundaries. This is a time for rejoicing. But you don't have to lose contact. You just have to concentrate on the person you miss and feel their energy once again.

Chapter 20: Another Secret?

There are those souls that have agreed to be together on earth to learn something from one another or to simply be together in their journey. However, because all humans have free will, then any human can change the charted path and the probabilities. The fact that my father and Lydia were close before my mother entered the picture makes me wonder. Does she and my father have unfinished business? After my father married my mother, he continued to "run into" Lydia in different ways and places. He was working as a civilian at the military base, became reassigned to a new unit, and there was Lydia sitting at a desk in the new unit. After two days, she was gone, and even though he would see her at different locations on the base, never asked her why she left. The fact that Lydia eventually married someone who also worked at the same base, made it easy over the years to keep track of her, even where she lived. Two years ago, Lydia's husband was gone and she was lonely and phoned my father. I can't imagine what thoughts passed through his head. He felt like she was giving him an invitation, but Mom was still here and he didn't pick up the ball. But Mom isn't here now and what will happen? Unfortunately, my mother also picked up the phone extension and heard their entire discussion. Ouch.

Chapter 21: Mid

Mid could only describe her childhood as horrid. Her mother was too unemotional, her father too strict. Their expectations of her were almost nonexistent. Mid was intelligent, much too intelligent to settle for the role of a woman in those days. She also was beautiful with smoky, dark eyes and a slim and lithe body being unusually tall in her day. This was a dangerous combination. She could manipulate the general population, but not her own parents. They just weren't interested.

When Mid was a teenager, her parents moved once again. The current schoolteacher had been renting a small house from her father. The teacher recognized Mid's brightness and offered to have Mid live with her so she could finish high school in the familiar school. Her parents too quickly agreed. This turned out to be a blessing for Mid for she was able to finish high school early and was ready to move on to college by the time she was sixteen. She hit a rock wall when her father refused to pay for college even though he could afford it. Her teacher encouraged her to apply for academic scholarships and she was awarded full tuition and room and board for a prestigious college about an hour away from her home.

Mid learned to never let an opportunity go by. She excelled in college not only in her academic life but also her social life. Men craved her seldom smiles and looked to her as a goddess. She thrived and became a celebrity at college at the age of nineteen, chosen as one of the thirteen most beautiful women on campus. She made a vow to herself to never have the kind of life her mother had experienced and rejected all her mother's ideals. She would succeed in life, she just knew it. Her hatred of her father pushed her forward and she would never forgive him for not treating her as a she felt he should.

Mid was finally charmed by a tall good-looking man from the same college, he with a French name. He was quiet but Mid took that as a sign of class. He was water to her fire. She and he would ride into the sunset together and become the perfect host and hostess and ooze wealth and class. There would be no children, Mid made sure of that.

As Mid matured with her marriage, she worked at the military base as a secretary. She found that she really didn't have to work too hard and could still charm her boss and have a social life. Her husband, to her disappointment turned out to be less than ambitious, although she drove him on to succeed, encouraging him to change jobs and take on more work. They lived in a small house near Kathryn and Thomas for a time but Mid had greater plans. She soon set her sights on a more prestigious neighborhood and convinced her husband of its value. Soon, they were building her dream home.

The home was beautiful. There was a rose garden and gardening became a kind of therapy to her, a way to reconnect with the soil and her nature. A gazing ball on a stone pedestal stood in the garden. The living room was a peaceful sky blue with a bright yellow sofa and white woodwork. The fire in the fireplace would sparkle and crackle and the clock would tick and bong on the hour. If you sat in her living room, you would have the sensation of time being suspended. And that is the way her life went. She had been so angry as a child, so resentful of her parents that all she did was an effort to eradicate their influence from her mind. By doing that, she forgot to live her own life.

She and her husband gradually drifted apart, with no children to bond them together. After retirement, her husband would get up in the morning, eat the same thing for breakfast year after year and then retire to the basement. In the basement, there were a few odd straight-backed chairs and a desk, along with some storage closets. He would stay down there an entire day, only coming upstairs to assuage his hunger and bathroom needs. What on earth would he do down there all day Mid would wonder. It was enough to drive her insane. There was nowhere to even relax; he would have to sit in a straight back chair all day long.

Mid would continue to participate in bridge groups and travel groups, alone if necessary and had a peaceful, if boring life. She never gained more than fifteen pounds as she journeyed through life and continued to be judgmental on all those women who gained weight after having children. She looked at children with disdain and only enjoyed one of Thomas' children because he spent the night at her house, the other children being too hesitant. She spoke to him and ignored the other two when with Thomas' family. She saw the changes in Kathryn as she lost her figure and grew older and was very pleased with herself, like a sly cat.

When Mid was in her eighties, her husband became ill with cancer. She tried to take care of him although it was almost physically impossible. Thomas stepped in to help, remembering the favors she had bestowed on him once upon a time. She grew restless and resentful and wondered why this was happening to her. Her husband grew increasingly ill and finally entered a hospice. After two weeks, he passed away and Mid was angry at the world. She was even more alone now; there was no other living presence in her house. She was angry at the hospice for letting him die; she should never have let him go there. She allowed no funeral, only a burial with no service. She watched the casket lowered into the soil and then drove away. There were no friends; there was only Thomas' family present.

The next year brought a steady decline in Mid's health. She became more angry and lost her memory. At times, she would drag a neighbor over to look in the basement to see why her husband was still down there when he was supposed to be dead.

She would call Thomas to come over and search the basement. At times, she believed her husband to be alive and at others she felt he was haunting her. She barely ate and lost weight. Kathryn tried to put their differences aside and would call Mid to see how she was. This stopped after Mid raged at her and told her to stop bothering her. Kathryn still sent meals over to Mid with Thomas when he would go to check on her. Mid nibbled on them but rarely said thank you.

Thomas had to call the police on two different occasions when Mid wouldn't come to the door. Once the police went in and found her on the floor and called the paramedics. After they stabilized her, she refused to go to the hospital and Thomas finally convinced her to go to the doctor at least. He was her only human contact from then on. He finally found a key and could go in without her permission and on one day he checked a few times and found no noise inside the house. Unfortunately, Kathryn would also be with him at this time and as they entered they knew she had gone on to meet her maker. Mid lay naked on the floor, with a carton of ice cream leaking down the counter. She never had the fist bite. She had been so dehydrated that she was burning up, pulled off all her clothes and was looking for something cool to assuage the heat.

Kathryn and Thomas were severely shocked at the sight. The police and coroner were called; procedures were taken care of. As per Mid's wishes, there was no funeral and no graveside service. Her casket was lowered into the ground, but her nephew, the one she favored, went against her wishes and said a verbal prayer to those of Thomas' family that attended. Then they drove away.

The Scene

It was finally over. The many flights back and forth to D.C., the constant hovering of reporters, the microphones thrust in his face, and the ever-present dark cloud hanging over his head. He was naïve in the beginning, thinking that he could bluff his way through. He also put a lot of faith in those surrounding him and thought they might actually have his best interest at heart. How ridiculous, it all seemed now.

He had aged ten years. What he had gone through was life changing. He would never be the same. After all the turmoil, he would be content to just sit in a dark hole in the wall and do tedious, menial tasks. Life just wasn't worth the risk of grasping it by the horns and trying to make it an adventure.

What is his marriage worth now? Will it ever be anywhere close to what he thought he had, to the pride he felt walking down the street with his wife on his arm? He loved to stare at her, at her poise, at her beauty. She enchanted him. Evidently, she had that effect on many, he mused, disgusted with himself.

At least he had been spared jail time. He would be returning home to his peaceful surroundings and eating regular food. But would he be returning to a marriage or just a relationship that was in limbo, or maybe with a truce declared. Dare he question her? Dare he even wish to learn the whole truth of the matter?

Chapter 22: Two Sides of a Coin

One gift my mother gave to me is that of standing up for myself. She never stood up for *herself* and I would see her stew and simmer in her distress after someone treated her unkindly or unfairly. This puzzled me greatly and I wondered why she did not respond to someone that had hurt her. She often just sputtered or walked away. However, the person would rarely get another opportunity to wound her because she just wouldn't put herself in a position to be hurt by them again. I could see the damage this attitude wreaked. Instead of clearing the air, she just let it suffocate her.

One of my aunts, one married to my mother's brother was an outgoing woman, vivacious and funny. She really didn't have that much confidence in herself, I could see, but my mother didn't see it the same way. This aunt would joke around, often at the benefit of someone else. One day, she said something and it hurt my mother. Rather than making a comeback, my mother walked away and never gave her the opportunity to hurt her again. My mother stayed angry at her for the rest of her life. On family reunion occasions, I would always enjoy my aunt immensely. My aunt became ill in recent years and had a lot of her own trials and tribulations to face. When my mother became ill, this aunt would call my mother frequently and come to visit, much to my mother's puzzlement. At my mother's funeral, this aunt was deeply saddened. I wonder what would have happened if my mother would have made a sharp retort to this aunt all those years ago. Would they all have laughed? Would my aunt have apologized? Would they be great friends? So much lost time and anguish in holding that grudge.

I could see this happening, a good lesson in life. I have learned to speak up for myself and not stay silent. I also know there is a right way and a wrong way to go about it. Don't back anyone into a corner without a way out and never place blame. If nothing else, I will have no regrets and no unfinished business when I leave this earth. I have become a diplomat because my mother was not.

Chapter 23: Needy

The theme of unfinished business keeps running through my life. Guilt is a powerful motivator and the desire to have no guilt is almost as powerful. What about all those stories you hear about never getting to say goodbye to someone because their life is snuffed out too early for some tragic reason? Do you ever get over the pain of not being able to tell them one last time that you love them? I can look back at so many things in my life and wish I had handled them differently, maybe been less judgmental, less angry, more open, more honest. Those wishes at least, have mostly to do with friends that I knew in my teenage years and in my twenties, not my parents. By my thirties, I was involved with my own children and less inclined to be so closely associated with friends and thus had less ties.

I had two saving graces in my teenage years, two important people in my life who enabled me to survive the simple pain I felt at being alive and also the feelings of loss I felt at not having a good relationship with my parents. One was my older brother and the other was my high school boyfriend. My boyfriend could have become my husband if I had followed the pattern known to many others. We dated ten years and then went our separate ways. Knowing someone this long makes them an indelible part of your life. We both tried so hard to be independent and mature in our relationship, the whole time being codependent and needy of the other, and not recognizing the patterns of less than perfect togetherness. We needed each other to survive.

I was only in eighth grade when I was standing in the lobby one day waiting to go into the lunchroom with my class. On the opposite side of the lobby was another class and at the front of the line was a young man dressed in dark gray flannel pants with a dark blue dress shirt. He had dark wavy hair and beautiful dark brown eyes with long lashes and just enough freckles to be disarming. I instantly knew he was the one I wanted. How could I know that? Most boys just didn't interest me with their "immaturities." But this young man had such an air of distinction about him; he looked confident and sure of himself, which made me quake inside. Anyway, I never did meet him that entire year and never even knew his name.

In ninth grade, a good male friend of mine sat behind me in Algebra class. He was a clown and was great fun. Sitting next to him was my dream man and my friend knew him! Ah, now the problem was trying to get an introduction without seeming too obvious and having my friend shout it to the world. Something worked right and soon I was talking to the "dream one." So I got to know the one I had my eye on and he ended up being even better than I imagined. He appealed to my sense of adventure for he would hitch rides everywhere and had a lot more freedom than I did. He even worked at a restaurant and had great stories to tell of the unusual people in the kitchen and the chef who was German. I fell madly in love and when our school field day arrived, we sat together and he even put his hand on my leg. Bliss! That summer he hitched rides to my house and we would go to the park, and do simple things that didn't cost any money.

Our relationship deepened and by the time I was sixteen he was driving and had his own car. My parents approved highly of him, after all he was working and didn't every parent want their child to have a job in those days? It didn't matter what kind or if you were happy. So, our relationship continued until one evening he didn't phone me as usual and that continued for a while. I was puzzled but not panicked until my friend the clown happened to mention that he had seen my boyfriend ice-skating with another girl at the pond. I was stricken with absolute terror. Nothing, and no one, had prepared me to deal with a difficult issue like this. Finally, after hearing more talk, my boyfriend called and told me that he "liked" this other girl now and that was that, we were finished. I had no say in the matter. Over a period of the next three weeks, I was in mourning. I couldn't eat, could barely function and I don't think my parents even noticed. I was dying and no one came to my rescue.

When I came to a point of not caring about anything anymore my boyfriend called back and said he made a mistake and wanted to get back together. I can still remember the phone call. I didn't really expect it, but somehow longed for it and also didn't ever want to speak to him again, all at the same time. Our phone was an old fashioned one that hung on the kitchen cabinet. If you wanted any privacy you had to pull the cord and wrap it around the doorway into the bathroom and shut the door on the cord. I was huddled in the dark in the corner of the bathroom with the phone. I don't even know why I took him back except that I really did love him. However, I was also wounded and from then on I told him things would be different. I then set out to show him I was in control and continued to date others alongside him. He would also date others at times, but I got so good at closing off my heart that I may have wounded others, which now I greatly regret. I regret my lack of sensitivity to *their* hearts. My heart actually grew harder while I was doing this. I became cynical after seeing how easily young men could be used.

What drew me to my boyfriend in the first place was a need to find someone to feel connected with, that could help me escape my unhappy life. My father at this time did nothing but ridicule me and my mother was lost in her own neuroses. My boyfriend also suffered from a loss of parental attention being one of five kids. His parents had a good partnership, however, and actually did things together like belonging to a square dancing group. They were often out for the evening and going to social functions, something I had no earthly idea that parents did. I never even had a babysitter growing up, not one! My parents never went out together, not to dinner, not to a movie, nada. So this seemed glamorous and added to his mystique. But actually, confident he was not. He was fighting for his survival like I was and practically drowning. He began to use casual drugs in high school but didn't really expose that to me because he would do them with the "guys," mostly older ones. In later years, he did alarm me because he also started to dabble in selling drugs, which always made me fear for him. I didn't know if someone would kill him or arrest him. I didn't know anything about addictions then, that people do that kind of thing to fill up a hole inside them. I just thought it was the 1970s and pretty normal.

Our relationship centered on working towards the future with very little real communication. We shared our goals, but not the depth of our feelings. I had never learned to communicate well and being an idealist, thought that loving someone meant that things would work out. If not, you just had to love them harder.

The end of our relationship came when he received his degree and decided to accept a job two thousand miles away without asking my opinion. I had been working on my career path already, having graduated before him. He never gave me an option or asked what I wanted, he just left. Very soon after, almost within a week, he began to ask when I was coming out to join him. I told him I wasn't too keen on that since he was the one who left, I was the one left behind. I was angry, too. It was the end for us.

Chapter 24: Kathryn's Heart

Dear Thomas,

I was truly in love with you when I married you. I thought we were special together and small things stand out. Like when you learned to bake cakes with me and we would make a homemade two-layer cocoa cake from scratch with luscious homemade icing made from a pound of confectioner's sugar. We watched every penny for a while. I knew you weren't happy working at the post office and working in jobs that you thought were beneath you. It wasn't in your nature to take a second seat to someone else. I understood that about you. Your father and mother were difficult to get along with but I thought that was the price I had to pay for happiness with you. I did enjoy playing games with your father. I thought that he liked me and in that there was protection from his anger for all of us. He didn't live long enough to know what kind of relationship would develop. Of course, he had mellowed by the time I met him. Your mother would never let you be totally mine. She gave me a lot of grief you know. When she wrote the letter about the twins and said their heads were deformed and was absolutely heartless, it broke my heart. The real problem was that she didn't want to admit she was now a grandmother. She was more concerned with her own image. And there was your sister, too. I could never live up to her standards. She never had baby spit-up on her shoulder! I don't think she ever even touched the children.

We struggled in those early years to build up some equity, to have a home and I tried so hard to make things nice for you. I worked all day and then cooked and cleaned. I don't know why I tried so very hard. Well, maybe I do. I wanted you to love me. I wanted you to love me so much that we would be together in harmony forever. I came to understand that I would never be enough for you. You wanted to socialize with other people. You wanted to play poker with the guys, get in the car and do trips to God knows where and go out to dinner all the time. But you wanted to go to the places that you wanted, not what I wanted. Did you ever ask me what I wanted? Did you ever say let's just stay home and listen to music and just be together? You would get angry if I didn't do what you wanted. Then I learned that Lydia was still working at the base when we were first together. Did you see her? Did you have lunch with her, casually run into her and just happen to pause in the hallway and chat oh so easily? But it wasn't you that told me. I learned it from bits and pieces along the way until I was so disillusioned that you could never hold a spell over me again. I began to withdraw and as such damaged myself. I didn't mean for it to happen that way, but it did.

With the children, I was happy again. There is no other feeling like it in the world than the unconditional love of a child. They were wonderful kids. I loved them with all my heart, and still do. Just because I am now on the other side doesn't mean I don't see everything that goes on. My energy is still hovering around you and I am aware of everyone's pain and everyone's actions.

You didn't enjoy the children but you tolerated them. Sometimes, I know you even did the right thing by them. I just wanted us to love one another and be happy. How naïve that now sounds. I didn't see that all of us had missions to accomplish and things to learn and work out for ourselves. After growing up in a household of conflict, I wanted to avoid it at all costs. But that veil is now lifted and I can see how things might have been different if I hadn't practiced some nasty self-abusive ways. It will take a while to forgive myself for that.

The grandchildren still need a grandfather. Just because I have passed over doesn't mean that they have released their need of you. You won't really let yourself see that, though. You will continue to be self absorbed and only concentrate on yourself. It seems more obvious that your children still need you but you also choose not to be aware of that. I am no longer the glue that held the family together. I am only vapor.

    I knew that you would run to Lydia after I was gone. I've always known and have lived with that knowledge for decades. You see, I knew you better than you knew yourself. I regret being bitter about it, for you couldn't have it any other way. You still have unfinished business with her. You haven't learned to open your heart yet in 85 years. So perhaps Lydia possesses the key. She will meet you on your own level and then what will happen? Will the fact that she won't care as much as you'd hoped force you to come to some realization? Time will tell. Perhaps there is still time for you to learn the lessons in love that you came to earth to experience.

    Don't make the mistake of thinking that I care about Lydia. You see I am vibrant and strong now and can see human life for what it really is, a learning ground for all the souls existing in this world. Where I am now, there is nothing but pure love. Hate and negative emotions have no place or meaning so I am restored. But I am still connected to the ones I loved and left behind, my children and their children and my brothers and their families. I will continually watch from my other dimensional world and wait with loving and open arms for their arrival here sometime in the future. And when you arrive I will nod to you and open my arms to your soul for maybe then, you will understand all that you are missing now.

    Your departed wife, Kathryn

Chapter 25: Torn

My brother used to tell me stories about knights. The theme was always about honor. Never lie, always be willing to die for those you love and sacrifice yourself if you have to. Honor was about doing the right thing no matter how much it hurt. Is there still a place for honor in our society? There are several different shades of honesty for most people. Most can't even be honest with themselves, let alone others. And doing the right thing often means doing the right thing more for yourself than the situation. But I have found that living my own life with honor is about winning the game of life fairly and about having no regrets, no guilt. Honor is also about finding my own place in the world and about doing some small part to heal it. I don't always fit in. I can't just let people make fun of others in my presence, I can't stand to see a person harmed deliberately and I can't abide dishonesty. And I still believe in love.

In the days of knighthood, the knights always had a lady who was their love interest, but one that wasn't really available to love openly. The purpose was for a knight to learn to love chastely and openly with no sexual reward. They would protect their love, converse with her and worship her, but not too closely. It is the kind of love that exists between two souls and not just humans. It's a love that seeks nothing in return but is openly given in generosity.

This conflict between idealism and what is real life has always been a challenge for me. Part of me expects everyone to do the right thing, but the right thing is not etched in stone. Every experience we encounter molds us into who we are, pushes and pulls us into shape of a human that still has issues, fears, challenges and hopes. I don't think that we ever reach a point where there isn't *some* challenge, for if we do then that is an exit point for the other side.

Chapter 26: Seriously?

When I was in my early twenties, fresh out of college and working at my first serious job, I found myself between boyfriends. Without much to do on the weekends, I took a few trips with my father to other cities to see the sights and mostly museums. My dad longed to travel and my mother adamantly refused. I was happy to have something to do. One night, at one of the hotels, my dad and I sat outside waiting for the sun to set. In white Adirondack chairs we chatted and my father opened up to me for the first time, surprising me.

He began to answer my questions and even though we were really talking, I still remember thinking *this can't really be happening. He's talking about his feelings?!*

He told me that when he and my mother met, they had so much fun together, they went to movies, dinner, all the things that most couples do. After they got married, he said that she began to pull back. I got the impression that there was another couple he enjoyed going out with and the drinks poured freely, but my mother didn't like them so it phased itself out. He said that she began to want children (she would have been past thirty by this time) so he "let" her have my brothers. After they were born, things changed drastically and she didn't want to do much of anything. Of course, I couldn't say, "You idiot, of course she was exhausted with twins," so I continued to listen. When he got to the part where he said he didn't want any more children but that my mom longed for a daughter, my ears perked up. Did he remember whom he was talking to? He gave me the impression that he grudgingly allowed her to have one more child, knowing that their marriage would be virtually over. The selfish bastard.

Chapter 27: Twisted

I had already made plans for my children and I to visit my parents when my aunt died. I had not seen her in years but had written to her faithfully on special occasions, feeling sorry for her lonely life. I knew she was a bitter and angry woman but I still felt sorry for her. She was responsible for a few memories in my life, ones that did shape my own destiny.

When I was a small child, she invited us over for dinner. She really was an excellent cook and because she was so much more formal than my mother, set the table exquisitely and the chandelier glowed above us. Her home was untouched by a child's hand and decorated well. Her foyer shone with lustrous black and white ceramic tile accented by a mahogany chest. Her kitchen had this really great little pass-through door on the counter for dishes to go back and forth between the dining room and the kitchen. Her kitchen had handmade turquoise cabinetry, the screened in sunroom stretched the length of the back of the house showcasing her blooming flowers and everything looked very elegant to me especially with her lemon yellow sofa. It would shape my ideas of the perfect home.

My aunt was very poised. Nothing shook her; nothing rattled her, unlike my mother who wasn't very outgoing. Mid cooked in a dress, one of those sateen things with a tight little cinched waist and a full skirt, kind of like the one Harriet Nelson wore on the television series, *Ozzie and Harriet*. When she laughed, her voice was melodic, although you would never have been able to coax a real belly laugh out of her. So, she did contribute to my seeing life outside of my family.

Mid and her husband would come over at Christmas, she dressed so well and her husband would be in a suit. My mother would prepare old-fashioned highballs and eggnog spiked with whiskey and I was allowed a very small sip. As I grew older, I became more aware of my mother's animosity towards Mid. Mid and her husband stopped coming over at Christmas with the excuse they didn't want to drive in the cold and snow. Offers to pick them up were rejected. I only saw her on very rare occasions.

After Mid died, I went over to her house with my father. He explained to me that the bank was the executor of her will and that she had left all her money to the college where she had known some satisfaction. She left my father, who had done so much to help her and her husband in their last years, two thousand dollars. She left my brother, her favorite, several thousand dollars and my other brother and myself nothing. I, wanting to have some part of her, paid her estate for some furniture so that I would have a piece of her. I don't know why I did it other than that it is a part of my childhood. It is a part of that little girl who looked in upon another world, one of more glamour and had high hopes for herself.

I knew that my uncle had spent hours in the basement alone and I presumed it to be to get away from Mid and her wrath. However, what we found in the basement was a surprise. We found stacks and stacks and more stacks of paper handwritten in ink mostly *about the weather*! He had written daily about the minutest details of the weather, including information about hourly temperature and precipitation amounts. It went back for years and years, with every hour of every day recorded in handwritten ink. I felt dizzy thinking about the time spent in this pursuit and wondered if he had lost his mind long ago. Some pages would talk about current events and then again, every tiny detail was put down in ink. It was mindboggling. There was never any opinion, any emotion. After reading some of the pages, it became too private a thing to read, kind of like watching a person's heart torn out, not by what the writer says, but from what he does *not*. There was agony in the work, a slow, mind-destroying angst.

We threw the years of accumulated work in the trash. What else could we do? I kept a few of my aunt's books, mostly classical works, but wanted them because they had dedications in the cover, in her writing. She had very few possessions that were a part of her. Her house felt sterile and unlived in, stale. It definitely felt smaller now, less grand.

She had lived the way she wanted and died alone. I often wonder how much she let her early childhood destroy any happiness she could have known. Children would have kept her involved in life, but God help any child she would have had. She wasn't meant to be a mother, or was she? Is it the innocent love of children that open our heart or does the heart already have to be open to receive it? I hope she got out of life what she needed to have.

Chapter 28: Marriage Guck

After I created my own social life again, my father still wanted to travel. We encouraged him to do some on his own, even if Mom refused to go. We would ask Mom where she would be willing to go and she would look hurt, put her nose up in the air and sniff as if the peons had asked her to eat dirt. Wouldn't most women be glad to get away? Not her.

So Dad did some of the auto club bus tours. You have to imagine how badly he wanted this to travel alone and ride in a bus all day. He seemed to enjoy them, met people along the way and took several tours. My mother began to steam and got more and more irate and her behavior became more neurotic. She actually seemed to flirt with Dad at times and at other times, ignore him. It was some weird married mating ritual that I could not even fathom.

My brother remembers that my mom went through my dad's souvenirs and saw a seating chart from an event, the bus, whatever. She saw that a woman sat next to my dad and that was it. She began a full out frontal attack to make sure my dad still belonged to her.

My dad told me that one day after lunch, they were discussing his trips and she fainted into his arms because she was so upset. I would have burst out laughing during the telling if it wasn't so sad. She just happened to swoon while you were right next to her and just happened to fall into your arms? No kidding.

So this kind of stuff continued until they came to some kind of understanding and actually moved into the same bedroom together again. Gasp. They had slept separately for *years*. Another time, my mother and father went for a walk and she tripped on the sidewalk and fell flat on her face. I think that was probably a plan that backfired, expecting my dad to catch her and play the hero, when he didn't notice until it was too late. She had a few bruises and scratches to show for that one.

They finally came to an agreement that she would go on a bus tour with him. They ended up doing two trips and she acted as though it was a sacrifice of the highest order. They toured through Florida and she didn't have anything good to say upon their return. They rode through New England on a fall leaves tour. Evidently, my mother didn't approve of the hotel choices, for when they were back in their rooms, after sightseeing for the day, she would hold a handkerchief to her nose the entire evening, saying that the hotels stank.

At stops along the way, she would refuse to leave the bus, not seeing the sights and sitting alone during lunches. My dad came back frustrated, confused, and a bit angry. My mother came back with her nose up in the air. They would never go sightseeing again. Their only travels would be to see their grandchildren. By that time, my mother (kudos to her at the age of seventy) finally got up the guts to set foot on an airplane and my dad had developed a fear of flying. Oy.

Chapter 29: The Rescuer

Anyone who's ever had a parent who reversed the roles so that the parent was often the child, forcing the child to become the parent or caretaker, knows what it is to be the "rescuer." I remember being only about five years old. For some reason, my mother was lying face down on my little twin bed with the blue patterned quilt, her hair in those old-fashioned brush rollers (man, those must have hurt) and crying. A real good boo-hooing. I remember standing at the end of the bed, tentatively saying, "Mommy?"

She continued to cry but allowed me to climb up on the bed and hug her. She told me that if she didn't have *me*, that life wouldn't be worth living. Whoa. Quite a load to carry for a kid. She held onto me for awhile, squeezing me till it hurt and my little kid brain thought that I'd better be on my best behavior for what might happen to my mom if I let her down?! That was a lot to carry around, but I did my best.

In third grade, another girl in my class had little in the way of toys and clothing. Her younger sister had very little, also. My best friend and I spent one weekend making yarn dolls and sewing a few tops and dresses for the dolls. I remember packing them into a shoebox to take to school and we gave them to the classmate's sister. The classmate ended up confiscating them from her sister and a big battle ensued until finally a teacher told us that a gift is a gift and once given, we have no control over what happens to it.

Throughout the remainder of my school years, I seemed to pick up misfits like some flotsam clinging to my clothes. I had shy girlfriends, social outcasts, boys with crushes, kids that had quirks and all kinds of issues that I seemed to overlook and just feel they were "misunderstood." I wanted to help bring out their "potential." I felt that I could see through to the "real" person and that I could help them. Why did I do this?

At the same time, one of my brothers, enmeshed in the history of the Knights of the Round Table was on his own mission of rescue. He seemed to be attracted to those who needed help and hung out with some odd ducks. As he got older and began dating, almost every one of his relationships was based on his feelings that he could be a "white knight." He would always tell the tale of her "sad" life where a previous boyfriend had abused her, she was misunderstood, she was destitute, she had gotten pregnant and been abandoned by the father of the baby, grew up unloved and on and on. He was to take her away from that life and she would appreciate him so greatly for that. Or not. All his relationships ended in emotional battles (and one restraining order) or, for his two marriages, divorce. He ended life, living alone with four cats, believing that a woman he had spoken to several times, was sending him a secret code through the phone lines, believing that she loved him, but that her boyfriend kept her from him.

This element of rescuing others is a form of codependency, I know now. You have to get some kind of payoff from it yourself or you won't be a party to it. The payoff is, of course emotional, feeling valued and needed. It's also a vicious cycle, for the relationship is never balanced and you end up being disillusioned when the person never lives up to your "idea" of them, they get sick and tired of you "helping" them or you just get sucked dry.

This whole dynamic also tends to skew your perception of love, you never feel unconditionally loved so you don't know how to accept it if you find it, you try too hard to be loved, you crave it too much and you end up in relationships where you feel used. It's hard to walk away from people who take advantage of you because "going the extra mile" is what you learned early on. What a conundrum.

Chapter 30: What Are The Odds

I'm sure there must be some statistics about how many families in the United States are touched by murder. Surely, it can't be that high. I know we have an alarmingly high death rate by guns, much higher than other countries but this is not the Wild West after all. But what sense does it make to be in a family that has been so touched by murder? First, my grandfather is a murderer, one that got away with his crime and evidently had no remorse. Secondly, a friend's mother is murdered and the person(s) who did the terrible crime are never caught. Then thirdly, my mother's oldest brother was murdered in a hotel room, stabbed multiple times by an unknown assailant. His is a strange story.

My mother's oldest brother was the prodigal son in the traditional sense. Coming from an immigrant family, he was the savior and pride and joy of his mother, my grandmother. She spoiled him so much more than the others. Her relationship was more of an awestruck girl towards him rather than a parent. She idolized him and expected great things of him, including looking after her in her old age, as any good son should do. This son had charm and charisma and the ladies eating out of the palm of his hand.

When he was in his teens, he smoked and drank and quit high school, which wasn't too unusual in those days. He went to work but had trouble holding a job. My grandmother would give him extra spending money, always buying into any excuse he had as to why he couldn't work or where the rest of his wages were spent. He soon got a girl pregnant and did the "right" thing by marrying her. As two lost souls that were put together, she also had lots of her own problems, health issues, insecurities and more, after all she was still very young. After the baby came, my uncle skipped town leaving my grandmother to look after his wife and their baby. Soon he came back, probably more because he needed money than because he wanted to take care of his wife.

He talked a great game and told his family about a great life and many jobs out west and he moved his wife and child with him to find his fortune. As the years past, my grandmother's heart was heavy with sorrow because her son never called to see how she was unless he needed something from her. It was a great loss in her life. Her other children were loyal and stayed by her side but they were not the ones she longed for.

In the years that passed, the son would be in town and not even call his mother, only calling his brothers when he was drunk and needed to be bailed out of jail. His brothers did their duty and then lost touch again for years at a time. My grandmother went to her grave not knowing his fate. No one saw the oldest, most honored son for almost two decades. Then, an article appeared in the paper about a murder victim, stabbed numerous times at an old hotel in the heart of the city where older, destitute people lived. My family saw the article and read it not even thinking they might have a connection to this person. No one saw anyone enter the apartment and no one heard any noise. There was a trouble light in each unit that the tenant could light up to show they needed help. The light was found on in the hallway.

The victim was identified as my uncle. My mother was understandably upset at the manner in which he died, however, she also felt that he had abandoned each of his siblings and his mother, and as such, deserved no real sympathy. It was a surprise that he had lived this long with his drinking habits and his love of excitement and his poor judgment. But murder is murder and no one deserves to die that way. There was never an arrest in the case.

So, here are two murders in my family. Isn't there some kind of statistic that says it just can't happen that way? How can a normal, dull family be connected with the most despicable acts known to humanity? Shouldn't there be something that protects us from that? I just don't understand.

Chapter 31: Spooky Stuff

About the age of ten, I discovered we owned an Ouija board. I don't know who bought it or why. My friend and I liked to play with it and we always asked it silly questions like the name of the men we would marry. I still remember the name it spelled and I have never met anyone by that name. We also asked it how we would die and that has yet to be proven, thank God! Of course, as the platen would move along the board and spell out things each of us assumed the other one was pushing it. We would accuse the other and each deny it at the same time. Then we took more mature views and decided that the other was pushing it but not doing it knowingly. One day, it was late afternoon or early evening as the sun was beginning to set. We were in my bedroom, sitting on the floor playing with the board and asking it the usual things when by coincidence we both attempted to catch the other one in the act of pushing the platen and removed our hands from it at the same time. To our astonishment, the platen continued to move by itself. It wasn't enough to have been given a shove, it just slowly and continually moved across the board. We were struck totally dumb and then as if a button were pushed, we both jumped up and ran screaming from the room. Neither of us wanted to re-enter the room and tried to tell my mother. Of course, no one believed us and everyone thought our excitement was just part of the game. To this day, I know that something else moved it, not either of us. It made me learn that there are forces greater than what we are taught in school. From this point, though, it was scary stuff, stuff to give you goose bumps on a dark dreary night. I didn't touch the Ouija board again.

I never lost my interest in the unknown, however, and continued to pursue studies of other worldly phenomenon. I read lots of books about many different subjects and had dark, heavy discussions about reincarnation, ghosts, intuition, channeling, mediumship and psychokinesis with those of similar interests. I met some psychic intuitives along the way, some good, some not so good, and some goofy. I've come to the conclusion that it's the same as finding a good doctor, you ask someone you trust for a referral and you don't answer just any ad in the yellow pages. I've also learned to trust my own intuition about who would work well with me. I take whatever they say with a grain of salt and decide if something they are predicting to happen would benefit me, or not, and then work to either make it happen or block it out. Kind of like going to a year's worth of counseling in one hour. You see what course the intuitive perceives as probabilities and then proceed from there, but never forget that no one is 100% accurate all the time. Free will exists in every realm.

I dabbled and learned, dabbled and learned for years. It was not something truly integrated into my life but more like a hobby. But finally, several years ago I had an experience that changed my thinking forever. I was in a class with Barbara Brennan as speaker/teacher. She is an ex-NASA scientist who was given the gift to channel an entity that gives information about how to live and why the world is the way it is. She went through a learning process herself to trust this energy and use it to help others. The class initially started out with no teacher. Barbara had been held up in a traffic jam and one of her teachers from her institute worked with the class until Barbara could arrive. The teacher told us about Barbara's background, that she was a scientist back in the 1960s and so I expected to see someone in her fifties. A beautiful young blond entered the room and I thought, oh no, they sent someone else because Barbara just can't get to the site. This woman appeared to be about twenty-six years old to me. Disappointment flooded me.

Then the stand-in teacher introduced the woman as Barbara Brennan. She was radiant.

Barbara explained what she would do and the entity she works with. When she began to speak after letting the energy fill her, it was with an entirely different tone of voice and inflection. Not only did she sound different, but her whole body was somehow different. Nobody, and I mean nobody, is that good of an actress. The words she spoke were with wisdom and knowing, from someone who must have lived thousands of years. It filled the audience with peace and love and if I had not experienced it first hand, I would never have believed it. She then spoke about the spirits she could see in the room and what they were doing and led us through exercises to be able to feel energy and work with it.

My body began to tingle and felt warm in spots as if someone were standing close to me but I couldn't see them. The little hairs on my arms stood straight up as if they sensed something. My entire body pulsed. If you have never felt this, I can't expect you to understand, it is still mindboggling to me that I had this experience. Afterwards, I would never be the same.

Walking away from this after working in a room with Barbara for eight hours is a little like going through a doorway and closing it behind you, knowing you can never go back to the exact same place again. Life had forever changed and it would take some time to accept what I had experienced and integrate it into my routine. What this did mean to me was that it was much easier to accept that when we die, we don't cease to exist but just travel to a higher level of energy and another dimension. It's like going to our version of Heaven except that there is no Hell. Our souls heal from our experiences on Earth and sum up our life as a learning experience and the soul decides if it accomplished what it set out to do, then plans for the next visit to earth and a new body.

So when we die, it is a time to be free of earthly restraints and know true, pure unconditional love again. It is a time to unite with other departed loved ones and to know kinship with them. The veil that is lifted after living life on earth shows each spirit clearly that their life on earth was nothing but an illusion and that true life is in spirit close to God. So I can be happy for my mother while still missing her terribly and know that she is still there, vibrant and alive in her energy form. I will see her again, of that I am sure.

So many people are afraid to believe in energy as a force in itself and it is always out of fear. Fear is such a good motivator that we use it to shelter ourselves in our lives. We are afraid that we will fail so we become overachievers, we are afraid we are unlovable so we work extra hard to make others happy. Fear is integrated into us and we use it also to make excuses. We are afraid that God will punish us so we try to be good. But if you can get beyond the fear and enter into the trust that God and his energy is there for each of us and that each of us is also a part of the energy, then we can transcend the fear and become part of the love of the universe. We can use the energy, read it, channel it and become one with it.

I didn't speak to my mother very much about my beliefs. I knew she was an intuitive woman but that she often chose not to trust her intuition or her dreams. So I honored her beliefs by not pushing mine on her. I wonder now what she thinks in her spirit form about if we could have shared more. Now she can see me purely as I am and I wonder if she thinks it is easier now to communicate. She let the medium know that "everything" I did for her in her final days was "all right" with the emphasis on right, meaning it ALL was right. What an incredible gift those words were to me. How would I ever have known otherwise that she was happy with what I did, that she was happy with *me*?

Chapter 32: Thomas and Kathryn, The End Years

Thomas knew something was wrong at the beginning of the summer. Kathryn just didn't have as much energy as usual and she seemed to be showing her age. She could usually walk farther, garden hours longer, clean the house without stopping and still stay up late to watch movies on television. Lately, she got tired so much easier. And she seemed to be gaining weight around her waist but not really eating. He had a vague sense of unease but wouldn't stop to consider the options. He proceeded with improvements to the house so that when he died, Kathryn wouldn't have to do any work but could live on there for years without any maintenance issues.

It was a shock one evening when Kathryn complained of a pain in her side. She rarely complained and didn't like doctors very much. She even took a pain reliever and she was known to go years without taking anything like that. The pain was so intense that she actually told him she wanted to see the doctor. The next day she did go to the doctor's office and they set up a battery of tests. The results were suspicious; she needed to see a cancer specialist.

Kathryn had decided to live to be a hundred years old, to see her great grandchild grow up so she didn't really expect anything to be wrong. Thomas was increasingly worried but tried not to show it. As the gravity of the situation hit him, he began to burst into tears at all different times of the day. His fear of crying was as great as his fear of being without Kathryn. If the children called and the tears came, he would hang up the phone or leave the room rather than cry in front of them.

On Friday the thirteenth, Kathryn and Thomas sat in the cancer specialist's office and received the sad news that Kathryn's cancer had already spread to fifty percent of her liver and the only thing they could do was try to slow its advance. Thomas wanted to know when it would happen, the end. The doctor hedged until Thomas continued to insist and so the doctor told them of an example of another patient, not giving a prognosis for Kathryn, mind you, but just as an example that he told the other patient two years. It was a grave disservice for Kathryn for she would only have seven weeks left.

Kathryn thought there would still be plenty of time to do some things she wanted to do, to say the things she wanted to say. Her children rallied around her and saw her whenever possible. Her brothers and their families sent cards and visited. She began to see that her family valued her. But she felt in her heart that Thomas' tears were not for her, but for himself. She believed he cried because his way of life was coming to an end, not because he would miss her.

Her appetite grew less and less. Her body swelled and her skin turned jaundiced. After five weeks, her son brought in the hospice people and she accepted that the end was coming. Still, she never cried.

Chapter 33: 1947
The Big Whammy- Secret Scandal

In 1947, newspapers still flourished, stylish dresses cost ten dollars and the United States was still unwinding from World War II and the fallout from hasty decisions, mistaken assumptions, corruption and the general panic that had taken place. Televisions hadn't invaded homes yet and people got their news from the radio, newspapers or movie reels played before the main feature in movie theaters.

That year, the movie *Miracle on 34th Street* debuted, the Cold War was in its infancy, the Roswell UFO incident occurred and the transistor, the Frisbee and the first "tubeless tire" were invented. People listened to Kate Smith and Arthur Godfrey on the radio, danced to swing bands and the "big band" sound and produced babies in record numbers, starting the baby boom.

Life began to take on more normalcy. Women returned from the work force and once again, stayed home while their husbands worked. The economy surged forward as many of the inventions that occurred for use in the war, were put into general use. Rudimentary computers, synthetic rubber and oil, plastics and advances in airplane technology created new industries. People moved to the suburbs and started a family centered lifestyle that included Little League and the Girl Scouts. The GI Bill of Rights provided veterans with money to go to college or get a mortgage.

However, since the war, a few whispers of unease began to flow into the optimism. The beginnings of the Cold War and a hearing in 1947 for investigations into communist activities in Hollywood contributed to this change in attitude. Now was the time when the government started to look for scapegoats or unscrupulous behavior that occurred during the war. The money spent on contracts to companies, people in positions of power, and those who received perks were all put under a microscope and the Senate convened the Congressional War Investigative Committee to rehash it all.

Howard Hughes, one of the richest men in the world and owner of Hughes Aircraft, was accused of taking over $40 million for aircraft contracts that never produced any airplanes. Hughes had been a child prodigy in engineering and golf, creating his own radio transmitter at eleven years old and golfing near par as a very young man. Everything he touched seemed to turn to gold. His life was glamorous and surrounded by Hollywood stars. The eccentric behavior that would become public after his death, of inches long fingernails and saving his own urine, was still decades away. He was called before an investigative committee and grilled on August 6, 1947 while dapper and charismatic. He also owned Trans World Airlines (TWA) whose main competitor was Pan Am at the time. Senator Owen Brewster, who convened the investigative committee, was rumored to be in alliance with Pan Am, so Hughes considered the investigative process to be something of a circus. It was also discovered that the hotel that Hughes stayed in, while in Washington, had microphones in the air ducts to listen to his conversations. The whole process of the hearings had a shadowy component.

Part of the discrepancy in the production of Hughes aircrafts centered on the Hughes Hercules, nicknamed by the media the "Spruce Goose" since the airframe and other parts were made of laminated wood. It became so famous that it can still be seen at the Evergreen Aviation and Space Museum in Oregon. It was a mammoth cargo airplane designed to carry hundreds of troops or tanks. People claimed it would never get off the ground but Hughes successfully flew it to a height of seventy feet, which he felt proved it would work. The government also needed to share the fault for not pursuing the production of the Spruce Goose. Government interest changed to the production of bombers, rather than cargo carriers, as the war heated up. However, Hughes Aircraft had still been paid millions to provide the aircraft and the senate committee demanded answers to appease their image. Hughes went into the hearings with a Congressional Medal of Honor awarded in 1939 and left with the image of a "mistreated war hero." With his experience in movie making, he had the hearings recorded and made the committee members look rather silly and vindictive. Perhaps that contributed to the senate committee's efforts to redeem themselves in the pubic eye later, with hearings concerning others who contributed to the mess in excess spending, including that of high-ranking government officials.

Everyone, with any possible complicity to Hughes, was called to testify. On November 12, 1947, one of those testifying was Major General Bennett Meyers, second in command of procurement for the Army Air Corps, which eventually would become the Air Force. He was based in Washington, D.C. General Meyers had been a commanding officer of Wright Field (which would eventually be combined with Patterson Field and become Wright Patterson Air Force Base, or WPAFB) before being moved to Washington to accept the new position at the pentagon. He was considered a "buddy" of Howard Hughes and a dining companion, although that friendship appeared to have soured by the time the committee hearings were held. At one time, Hughes was supposedly buttering Meyers up to keep a direct line into the government and told Meyers he would like to have him run one of his companies after the war. Meyers was also the owner of Aviation Electric Company, located near Wright Field in Dayton, Ohio, which received wartime contracts for airplane parts for allegedly four times what they were worth. During the war, because of the way the company was set up, no one publicly knew that Meyers was actually the owner of Aviation Electric.

Meyers testified during the Hughes hearings that Howard Hughes had asked him to offer an under-the-table bribe of $150,000 to the Legion of Decency to lift a ban on a racy movie, *The Outlaw*. Hughes had produced the movie, but had not been allowed to show it in New York, because its content was deemed inappropriate for the times. Hughes denied that he tried to coax Meyers into bribing the Legion. Hughes then testified that Meyers had asked Hughes for a loan of $200,000 to help finance a $10 million bond deal. That was, coincidentally, just before Meyers signed a contract for the government awarding Hughes a $22 million deal for aircraft. Meyers claimed it was a lie and said the bond deal was financed with a bank loan. They both pointed fingers at the other. By this time, with the war over, Meyers realized that Howard Hughes was not about to offer him a job and was ready to say anything he wanted to about Hughes, with no loyalty to the man whatsoever. No longer needing one another for the power or money they could offer, they were free to go after each other's throats.

Meyers was also questioned about his ownership in aircraft companies and he replied that any stock he held was actually in his wife's name. He ranted that he was a patriot and was doing his duty just to win the war.

At the hearing for Hughes, it is important to note that before Meyers' testimony, supposedly Meyers had gone to lunch and had several cocktails, and ignoring the slogan of the times "loose lips sink ships," he happened to mention Aviation Electric during his time on the stand and triggered an avalanche of an investigation into his own business interactions. He was sunk. What came out of all this was the biggest question of all: *what was the Deputy Chief of the Army Air Corps, General Meyers, a recipient of the Distinguished Service Medal and Legion of Merit, the man who ran and awarded companies $60 billion* *dollars in aircraft contracts from the government (which could make companies millions), doing as an owner of one of those same companies?* This was a direct conflict of interests and a violation of government policy. Just as letting a "fox in the henhouse," letting the man that could dish out contract awards in the millions own his own company that received some of the contracts, was extremely disturbing to the reputation of an officer, the air corps and the government.

Hidden in General Meyers' government file, buried deeply, was an anonymous letter addressed to the military that been sent much earlier. It detailed Meyers' involvement with the "dummy" company of Aviation Electric. The letter stated that the writer was in the military and feared "vindictiveness" if his name were known. The writer and "snitch" were never revealed although speculation existed. The letter was kept hidden and didn't come to light until later in the hearings. Whoever received the letter initially made the choice not to pursue an investigation and not let it be examined too closely. This letter would come to light during the hearings into Meyers' activities and those involved in ignoring the letter would also be on the hotseat.

At the time of the hearings, Meyers lived on an eight-acre estate with eighteen rooms in Long Island along with his third wife, the actress Ila Rhodes, nineteen years his junior. He was known for living a high rolling lifestyle and enjoying his share of poker and cigars. This lifestyle certainly supported the appearance of possible illegal activity. All this money had to come from somewhere.

The Senate Committee began to investigate Meyers and called the president and vice president of Aviation Electric to testify. Everyone, scrambling to protect themselves, and Meyers to protect the fortune he had amassed, told stories that were very scandalous for 1947.

The president of Aviation Electric originally lied about his role in the company. He testified that he owned the company and that Meyers had no interest in it other than to loan the company money. By then, the Brewster Committee was headed by ex-Detroit prosecutor Homer Ferguson. Many of the investigators were former FBI agents. The president was pulled aside privately and spoken to by Chief Counsel William Rogers and sub-committee counsel Francis Flanagan. After that, with the advice of his own lawyer, the president wrote a letter to General Meyers claiming he truly believed Aviation Electric was legitimate and had no part in any criminal activity. The general told him the letter was foolish and tried to get the president to backtrack and urged him to tell a story that the president had a gambling addiction to explain where all the money went and to stick with that story.

The president then turned on Meyers and let it all come out. He testified that he was ordered to perjure himself by Meyers about his position as the "dummy" president, about kickbacks and the price rigging of orders.

General Meyers held his ground and as the tide began to turn he used an ace to try and upset the testimony. Meyers, knowing full well the sensationalism that would result, testified that the president's wife had been his (General Meyers) girlfriend with the "full knowledge and consent of her husband" and that was the real reason he started the company, to keep her nearby. Back in 1947, the standard was chivalry and to never "dishonor" the reputation of a lady, whether it was deserved or not. To say what he said in front of the citizens, the nation and the world was an enormous shock and quoted as setting a "precedent" for the military. Honor was still very much the standard. The scandal that a high ranking military officer would have a mistress who just happened to be married and all of it happened with her husband's knowledge and consent, well, that was huge. That started an ever-increasing emotional storm in the hearings and the media.

As testimony unfolded, the testimony told in front of Congress and the world was that Meyers carried on a five-year affair with Mildred Lamarre, his married, attractive secretary while at Wright Field, *with* the permission of her husband, Bler. The general and she met in 1936 while Mid was in her twenties, working at Wright Field. Although the general was well into midlife, his power would have been attractive to her. Her beauty, confidence and husky voice would have been exciting to him.

The general, at the time of his supposed relationship, was chief of the Budget Section at the Dayton, Ohio base when Mid became his secretary. Mid's husband, her college beau, was blond, good looking and the complement to her fire. He was mild mannered and calm. Mid was ambitious and feisty.

Whether it was through connections with the general or not, in 1939 Mid and Bler ended up in California so Bler could work for Douglas Aircraft in Santa Monica. Bler left for his job in the spring and Mid joined him later in the summer, spending several months alone in Dayton. The story was that Bler went to California to keep his wife away from the general.

By the winter, the general visited the couple in California and convinced them that returning to Dayton would be a good idea. The general now had a position open as president of Aviation Electric, a job that he offered to Bler. The job, of course, was a setup, but a setup to what? Did the general really enjoy their company so much that he wanted to do them a favor? Or was it Mid's company he enjoyed? Or did he just know that Bler would make a good patsy?

The salary settled on was $30,000 a year (equivalent to $320,000 today), which was outrageous for a young man in his twenties and with no real experience. Bler would testify that all but about $2000 was kicked back to the general in cash, showing a paper trail of a large salary but nothing else as to where the money went. The fact that Mid and Bler's house was modest and they didn't own extravagant luxuries would bode well for his testimony.

Aviation Electric set up shop in Dayton with five employees and some machines to produce electrical sub-assemblies. The price for the sub-assemblies would bring in a profit of four times the cost to produce.

Bler then brought in his brother-in-law, Thomas Readnower, a young college graduate as the Vice President of Accounting for a salary of $18,500. Supposedly, 90% of that was kicked back to the general. They hired Kathryn Weaver as their bookkeeper. Thomas would ride through Wright Field in the general's Cadillac and would be "lucky" enough to win the wartime lotteries that doled out refrigerators and automobiles, having some of the most sought after luxuries of that time period. He was also "lucky enough" not to be sent to fight overseas when drafted, but was stationed back at Wright Field after basic training. When drafted, he was already working at Aviation Electric.

Meyers began to be promoted and rose through the ranks. By 1942, he was transferred to Washington, D.C. and lived in a luxurious apartment. Meyers began to recommend Aviation Electric to his friend, Lawrence Bell, who owned Bell Aircraft. Bell would later testify that he subcontracted over $1.5 million with Aviation Electric.

A decorating bill of over $10,000 for Meyers' Washington apartment was paid for by Aviation Electric. It was also at this time that the general began a relationship with the movie actress, who became his third wife. The general gave the order to Bler to hire her father for a position as Vice President of Operations although the father's previous job was as a bus driver. The father was to be paid $1000 per month.

World War II was still raging and as the high command of the Air Corps heard rumors of high-ranking officers having stock or interests in companies receiving wartime contracts, word went out to all of them to sever ties with these companies. By then, the general had transferred all the stock in Aviation Electric into his wife's name.

As the Congressional Hearings against Meyers proceeded, photographers swarmed around Mid and Bler, both very photogenic. Pictures showed them exiting the hearings, sometimes with Thomas, smiling broadly and with Mid wearing a fur coat. They all looked as though they had just been to a Broadway play, rather than testifying in front of a Congressional hearing. Articles would be featured in *Time Magazine*. Cigar smoking Meyers, bold as brass, acted confident throughout the process. Meyers said that a Cadillac, the $10,000 used for decorating the general's apartment, a $700 radio as well as other items were "gifts" to the general for his support of the company.

During the hearings, General Meyers met Thomas at a Washington hotel and tried to get him to back up the gambling story he wanted all of them to support, that Bler wasted all the company profits, and Thomas, who refused to go along with it, is quoted as saying, "It sounded too ridiculous."

General Meyers' father-in-law, the former bus driver, was called to testify. Fumbling with notes, Mr. Curnett had difficulty answering questions until the counsel looked at the notes and found that they had been typed by his daughter (General Meyers' wife) and Curnett's wife and cast light on whether Mr. Curnett was going to testify truthfully. Finally, Curnett stated that one of the reasons he left the company was because he found Kathryn and Bler in each other's arms. So, here you have Bler, whose wife is allegedly having an affair with the general, Kathryn who is the bookkeeper in the arms of Bler but by 1947 was married to Thomas. And by the way, Kathryn was married to someone else at the time of Mr. Curnett's observation. Whew. Hard to keep all that straight!

Curnett's testimony had a backlash, however. In those days of honor as the standard, no one could believe that yet another woman's honor had been impugned, and because these men were using these women so terribly, the hearing committee refused to accept it. It backfired and looked very poorly for the general.

Bler, back on the stand at the hearings, referred back to the General's testimony about Mid being his girlfriend of five years and said that, "There weren't enough words in the English language to describe the depths to which he (General Meyers) has sunk. He has instituted a smear campaign against myself, my wife, Mr. Readnower, his wife, and in the testimony that Mr. Curnett gave, it is apparent that he wanted Mr. Curnett to do the same thing. And it is absolutely without foundation. It is my sincere hope that this Committee will make General Meyers crawl out of this room on his belly like the snake that he is."

Mid took the stand and the general smirked and winked at the lawyers. She said that when she disagreed about telling the story Meyers wanted her to tell the committee, he told her she would be very foolish and to "just wait to see what happens to her." She denied any improper behavior and said Meyers' testimony was "bare-faced lies."

Pictures would be featured on the front page of nearly every major city's newspaper about the "scandalous" allegations concerning Meyers' mistress. Headlines would shout, "Meyers Blames Woes on Love", "Parents Brand Love Story 'Lie'", Lamarre Denounces Meyers as 'Liar, Snake'", "Meyers Lied for 'Revenge', Mildred's Mother Tells News", "Readnower Salary Went To Meyers, Letter Coverup Blamed On Air Force Leaders", Lamarre's Wife Brands Meyers Liar", and so on and so on. Soon, the media swarmed on the small, average home owned by Mid and Bler. The newspapers printed pictures of their home, Mid's picture from Miami University, pictures of the couple leaving the hearings, pictures of Mid, Bler, Thomas and Kathryn together, pictures of Mid and Kathryn and even a picture of Mid's collie. Somehow, Kathryn was left out of testifying and was only mentioned in passing in the newspaper articles, although she posed in pictures with Mid for a show of support.

Reporters found Mid and Thomas' parents in Kentucky and were invited in for refreshments. (Who does that?) Mid's mother said her daughter begged Bler to tell the truth at the hearings and that Meyers brought Mid into it to get revenge when Bler told the truth. They called her "the soft spoken mother." Really? I can only remember a rather opinionated, prominently spoken self-righteous woman. Soft spoken, definitely not.

In this case, the photos of the home worked out well. It showed that the Lamarres were not living extravagantly and were in fact, quite modest. There was no evidence that Bler had ever collected a huge salary. However, the general was living beyond the means of a military man and flaunting his wealth.

Citizens wanted blood. Organizations such as Amvets called for the revocation of the general's medals, others called for a court martial. General Arnold came out of retirement and said that Meyers had disgraced the uniform and that he was grateful that others had found "a rotten apple in our barrel."

Mid filed a slander suit against the general which didn't go anywhere, the general was indicted on income tax evasion and other charges. Bler was tried for perjury and given a sentence of 1-3 years, suspended with probation for two. Bler was a free man. Bler ended up working for Standard Oil, starting as a gas station attendant and worked his way up to an office job. Meyers would serve time in prison, sentenced to up to five years and lose his pension and everything else, including his third wife, the actress. Rumors later swirled that when released, he changed his name. The money he amassed in the wartime contracts? Unknown.

After the war Thomas went to work at the Post Office and generally hated his job. Thomas was then approached with an offer to return to Wright Field as a procurement officer in civil service. What part his testimony played in receiving this job is unknown. He would specialize in procuring parts for missiles and airplanes and rise to become one of the highest-ranking civilians on the base by the time of his retirement twenty-five years later.

Mid and Bler would remain married and childless for the rest of their lives, living a rather quiet and solitary existence, rarely traveling but enjoying their collies and a lovely home they built later.

Chapter 34: Miami University, 2010

I walked into the building that housed the private collections bestowed to the university. There were glass panels and doors that revealed an area that resembled any library with tables and a librarian sitting at the front desk. I gave them my name and since they were expecting me, they wheeled out a triple-shelf cart with all the items they stored in a climate-controlled room. Asked to put everything in a locker, including my purse, and don white gloves, I was then invited to take my time and look over all the items with only a pencil and paper allowed to take notes.

I chatted with the librarian and was told that the person cataloguing all my aunt's items was very intrigued with the events that had gone on. It wasn't just a job to her but a story. Yes, I agreed, it was some story!

Back in those days, it was nothing for a newspaper to print your address and yes, even show a photo of where you lived and in this case, an aerial view of the house where my aunt and uncle lived. Their house is shown in both an aerial and full frontal view, a rather charming white frame house with a second story and window boxes. Did they really put a plane or helicopter in the air just to take that picture? Talk about lack of privacy, but I guess people were much more respectful then and you didn't expect to be stalked.

In 1947, Dayton, Ohio still had three newspapers: the *Dayton Journal*, the *Dayton Daily News* and the *Dayton Herald*. On November 21, 1947 it was a front-page kind of day for my family on all three. The *Daily News* described my aunt as the '33 Miami University beauty; the cover depicted her college picture with wavy, black hair, beautiful features and a soft furry collar of some sort. My uncle was pictured at the hearings in front of a big desk-style microphone. General Meyers is seen scratching his face while testifying. The story rakes General Meyers over the coals for signing a false affidavit about a Cadillac purchased by Aviation Electric for the general's use. It was significant because of the wartime freeze on new cars, needing the metal for wartime equipment. They also grilled him on a decorating job for his wartime apartment that cost $10,000, paid for by Aviation Electric. The paper went on to say it included air conditioning and a radio worth $700. In today's dollars that would mean they spent over $104,000 to decorate an apartment and paid over $7000 for a radio. That was living high on the hog for a military man.

My aunt had apparently saved all the articles about 1947 that she could get her hands on. There were full front pages of the newspapers with her picture featured prominently. Many, I had already seen online but some were still a surprise. There were also love letters between her and Bler as well as their beautiful wedding photo of an exceptionally sophisticated and elegant Mid. That was hard to imagine for someone who had only seen their relationship in later years. There was not enough time to secure copies of everything but I paid the librarian to copy what time allowed.

Shocking to me were the photos of my father and mother together sitting beside my aunt and uncle in a show of solidarity. In not one of these photos is anyone looking remotely worried, but they appear very pleased with themselves. Even my mother looked at ease and smiling. Very odd. Where had that woman disappeared to? Were they basking in the attention of celebrity-hood?

Chapter 35: Upside Down

My mother ended up being very close to correct; my dad sold our childhood home, bought a condo within a block of his old college girlfriend, and spent much of his day (if not all day) with her. She wanted to get married but he refused. She often asked him just what had happened all those years ago, just what did she do wrong. He wouldn't tell her that he had just been swept away by his desire for someone else; he remained mum.

My brother, browsing the Internet one day, "googled" our last name and stumbled upon an article about the 1947 hearings. He brought the article over to my dad's condo, had a small discussion with my dad about it, and left the article there. My other brother, visiting my dad on another day, took the article home and did his own search of the web, turning up more articles. Then, he called me and told me that he found some information implicating our uncle and father in something big.

I remember those first few feelings of disbelief and then the nagging remembrance of those times when my mother would say that she had some things to tell me, things that wouldn't be said until after my father had gone to meet his maker, implying they had something to do with my aunt and uncle. She would look distressed and I dismissed her words due to the poor relationship between she and my aunt, and the cold war between she and my father. I remember very specifically sitting on a stool at the kitchen counter, my mother standing across from me and she was almost wringing her hands as she told me she needed to tell me some "things" after Dad was gone. I wished I had pushed for more back then. I wish I would at least have had a glimpse of what she wanted to tell me. What I wouldn't give to hear her perspective now.

I loved to do research on the Internet and found some extremely valuable sites for old newspapers and genealogy. For two weeks, I existed in a state of distress, amazement and disbelief as I found city after city's newspapers with front page articles, with my aunt, my uncle, my dad's shining faces grinning at me from before my birth. The *Washington Post*, the *New York Times*, *Time Magazine* and every major and minor newspaper in the country knew about this! Holy Shit! My parents were notorious. It wasn't just the shock of knowing something that the rest of the world had known, was hidden from me, their daughter, it was the after shocks, those moments of near hyperventilating because I soon realized that I had to question everything I had ever been told.

It took me awhile to wrap my head around this, for me to acknowledge that this really happened. I felt as though I were in the Twilight Zone. Where had my boring, ordinary, dull uninteresting family gone? Oh, and by the way, did I mention that while doing all these Google searches, I also pulled up the murder accusations against my grandfather for killing my grandmother's first husband? Because of the newswire services, this little tidbit also made it into *The Washington Post*.

During the 1947 scandal, even my grandmother featured prominently on front pages, defending her daughter's honor. There was *her* picture, years younger than the grandmother I knew.

The shock and pain of all this had much more far reaching effects than just finding out the kind of family I came from, for now I began to question everything I had ever been told as a child and an adult. Confronting my father, he stood in his condo living room, looking almost gleeful, saying he wondered when we would find out. That was it? He was proud of all this? He got one passed us? Oh, no, no, no.

I kept asking questions, I kept trying to find out what he had been thinking when involving himself in something dishonest and risking jail time. He said that he used to take the money paid for the dummy contracts, cash the checks and then get on a train to Washington. He would drop in at the Pentagon and hand the money over to General Meyers. He said that the salaries stated in the hearings that he and Uncle Bler supposedly received were actually inflated, too, so that more money went into the General's pockets. He didn't seem to feel any remorse, no doubt about his role, nothing but a kind of self-satisfied smugness that I couldn't fathom. What happened to your insistence on honesty, Dad? What happened to never, ever telling a lie? What happened to all the punishment for doing anything remotely like fibbing?

You've got to love the Internet, as more and more newspapers scan their ancient journals, the more they are available online for all to see. University private library papers, front pages of various papers and even old newsreels of Congressional Hearings, all right there, in your face. EBay and Historic Images are even selling old press photos of my aunt and uncle. Sheesh.

Chapter 36: Breathless

I could never have imagined the shock and sheer breathlessness of finding my parents, aunt and uncle on the cover of every city's newspaper in the U.S. The family I thought I knew, the boring, ordinary, life going tick-tock, tick-tock was blown to bits. Not only blown away but in such a way as to be the ultimate betrayal. An event, so tumultuous, so life changing, so untimely, was totally hidden from me. A huge part of my parent's lives were stripped bare and shown to be nothing but lies and fluff. How could I ever now believe anything that had been told to me? How could I ever believe anything that had come from them? The pain, the anguish? Ahh, unimaginable.

I asked my dad, did she do it? Did my aunt carry on an affair beneath her husband's nose, with his knowledge, with his consent? He got that look again, the one where I knew he would never tell me the real truth, the one where his lips screwed up, and he wouldn't look straight at me and said, "I hope not." What the hell does that mean? He had to know the truth to that, he was there, he lived through it. He was riding around the air base in the general's Cadillac and he didn't know? No, I know he knew, but he wouldn't admit to the shame.

And somehow, I got the feeling that he wrote that anonymous letter about the general's involvement in Aviation Electric based on the same expression on his face.

Chapter 37: Their Own Words

I asked both of my parents to write about their childhood so that I could keep their memories safe. What follows is what they wrote:

In Kathryn's Own Words:

First recollections are of a dark double house with a railroad running practically in the backyard. When coal trains would slow up, men in the neighborhood would climb up and throw down lumps of coal to take home for their stoves. Mom didn't want Pop to do this as it was very dangerous. The train would jerk and speed up and the men had a hard time climbing down. Also, there were railroad detectives on some trains and they would arrest the coal thieves. That meant jail and fines if they were caught.

There were several men boarders for a while. They ate so much it wasn't worthwhile to keep them. I can remember one of them tossing me up to the ceiling and letting go and then catching me. My screams brought my mother into the room and she gave him a piece of her mind. It was rough making ends meet in those days. There were no toys for any of us. Most of the time, I looked out the window and watched other children playing outside. My mother didn't want anything to happen to me so I had to stay inside. There were lots of men "riding the rods" (hitching rides on trains) to go to different cities to look for work. Sometimes they would go from house to house looking for food and clothing. Some were pretty scary!

After things settled down, my parents found a house to buy about a block away and right next to the grade school. Our back gate opened out to an alley and the school was there. The house was newly built but someone didn't think ahead. They had put gas lighting into the house whereas electricity was being used everywhere. The first thing Pop did was to change it to electricity. The house attracted my parents because of the school being so close and no streets for us to cross in getting there.

In first grade, I had a nice teacher and we learned everything from cards the teacher held up and we all recited in unison. To me, going to school opened up a new world. Even though I was very shy and timid, I was eager to learn. In the second grade, sometimes we were asked to bring in money for some craft. One in particular was weaving a hammock for a doll. I couldn't bring in money, but the teacher let me make one anyway. We just didn't have any money for extras. The school would have sales to make money for some special items they needed and sold caramelized popcorn patties and soft pretzels often. I believe pretzels were about two cents each and, once in a while, Mom would have me buy five and that was a deluxe treat. We had other moneymaking campaigns but I was never permitted to go door to door to sell. That was just as well as I am sure I would never have gotten up the nerve to even knock on strange doors.

I can remember how well I liked spelling, arithmetic and reading and how hard I worked to memorize my spelling. If I missed any words on a spelling test, I would be miserable and study harder. After I learned to read well and a branch library was opened in our neighborhood, the girl next door took me there so I could get a library card and take home books to read. That was so wonderful, especially during school vacations. I spent all of my free time reading and made many trips to the library during the week.

One thing I remember about the school was there being three frame buildings besides the brick building. I remember being in the frame buildings for first grade but not long after that, the frame buildings were torn down for a playground. Of course the playground was only a large area with gravel on it, no playground equipment of any kind. The kids ran around and played tag or shoved each other. Sometimes, the kids threw stones over our shed roof and they landed in our yard. Mom would go to the gate and yell at them to quit doing that. There was a lot of that, also the neighbors complained too. After school, the children had to walk past our house when going home and didn't care where they walked. We had a fence put across the front of the lot and hedges. The other neighbor did the same. Being close to school had advantages and lots of disadvantages. The backyards were all fenced in solidly so the kids couldn't climb the fences. Once in a while a bold kid would manage to get into our neighbor's yard and the old lady there would go out with a broom and swat him one, and he couldn't get out of the yard fast enough. There were six girls living there, all older than me. The youngest, Marie, was always advising me on what to do. When it came time to go to high school for the seventh grade, I was scared stiff. My oldest brother never bothered about me or cared to break me into a new school. Marie went with me and showed me around, as I had no close girlfriends. After that, I found someone to walk home with after school who lived in the neighborhood. At the school, there were students from every nationality. North Dayton had various sections where they lived. One area was the Hungarian Village or as some called it the "Hunky Colony." Close by was an area for the Polish people, Lithuanian and German people. Each group had their own Catholic church. Most of us walked to school. A few rode streetcars. I went to the Lithuanian church until I was about nineteen. My brother and I went to early mass every Sunday, even though our parents didn't go. We had to learn Catechism after church from the nuns who came from another parish but after the priest left and another arrived, the new priest took over the teaching. He was so mean and had no patience with children. After First Communion we quit Catechism (he was Lithuanian).

A man in the parish thought it would be a good idea for the children to learn to read and write in Lithuanian. I was interested so I went in the evening along with some others. It wasn't long before the classes got so unruly the poor man had to call it quits. However, I feel like I did get a lot out of it for the short time I went. I wrote letters to my mother's family in Lithuania, probably with poor spelling but they got the message. One boy was studying English so he tried to write in English but World War II brought the correspondence to an end.

I was "confined" to our neighborhood for so many years that I didn't know my way around very many places other than school and church. In the seventh grade, one of the teachers drew a map of downtown Dayton with the streets marked and asked us to tell her where various business places were located. I was at a loss. I had gone downtown occasionally with my mother but had no idea what streets we were on. Most of the time, we went to the Farmer's Market and then back home. Usually, she went alone on Saturday and I was supposed to scrub the kitchen floor while she was gone, also the middle room. I always laid down newspapers on the floor after it was dry so it wouldn't get tracked up before Sunday. Sunday was a day of rest.

After I was old enough and could add well, I went to the grocery, Piggly Wiggly, about a block away with my younger brother. He pulled the wagon while I got the groceries. The clerk waited on us behind the counter and got everything we asked for. After I paid, we put the groceries in the wagon and took it home. I don't remember how long I did this. After buying groceries, I went across the aisle to the meat counter to buy meat. The countertop was almost as high as I was. I had to stand on tiptoes to tell the butcher what I wanted and pay for it there. So many times, I was overlooked since I was a kid. I usually had some message to give the butcher like I wanted half a regular smoked ham, not sugar cured, a whole pork loin sliced, etc. I also went to a small grocery on the other side of the "tracks" run by a Hungarian. He specialized in better quality meat and usually I bought pork shoulder or chuck roast (message to him from my mother- not to cut close to the neck for chuck). My father always walked to work and left the house early in the morning, taking his lunch. Most of the time it was thick slices of ham on dark rye bread, the round loaf kind, or salami on rye. He drank water at the foundry with his lunch. He was a molder at the Iron and Brass Works and worked there until he retired. That was a hard job pouring molten brass or steel into molds. Dirty and hot! After working in the heat of the foundry, summer heat at home didn't bother him. He sat in the double lawn swing he had made and enjoyed swinging. Sometimes, I would sit with him and he would tell me stories. The one that always impressed me was his admiration of the Russian Cossacks. They would come into the Lithuanian village where he had lived and were on beautiful horses and I guess they did things to impress the people. He never talked about his family much that I can remember but two of his brothers came to America with him. He kept in contact somewhat with his brother, a bachelor who died. The man had worked in the coalmines and died penniless. He lost track of his other brother. I believe they had a disagreement of some sort. Pop also had other relatives that came to Dayton but I could never quite understand the relationship, probably cousins.

Mom had her passage paid by an uncle who had come to America years before. She was the youngest in her family so he brought her to Dayton to live with his family when she was about sixteen from Lithuania. After she got here, she went to work at a cigar factory rolling cigars, which she hated. A lot of young men from Lithuania were single and looking for women to marry so it wasn't long before she got married and had children.

In the good old summertime, Mom would put her two zinc washtubs on the wringer under the grape arbor where it was cooler. I had a scrub board in the soapy water and would rub the clothes on it, put it up to the wringer rollers and my brother would turn the crank and they would plop into the rinse water that had bluing in it. We would swish the clothes around and then put them through the wringer again and hang them on the clothesline. The soap was either Fels Naptha or homemade lye soap. The white clothes were boiled in a copper boiler on the gas stove in the summer kitchen. The steam in that little kitchen was hot! The bathroom was next to the summer kitchen. My father had added those two rooms to the house when the Board of Health ordered all outhouses closed and indoor plumbing used. I don't remember how old I was when that happened but I remember taking baths in the washtub behind the heating stove in the "living" room on Saturday afternoons. Pop had a long bathtub put in so he could be in it and soak all the foundry dirt off. Mom thought the tub would waste a lot of water so thought the kids should use the same water. I was supposed to use my brother's bathwater but she couldn't get me into that tub for all the threats and arguments. She realized it was a losing battle so she decided we could use our own water but were not allowed to use too much. To save electricity, everyone went to bed early during the winter. In the summer, we were allowed outside to play after supper. As a rule, a bunch of the kids in the same block would go together and played games: Hide-and-Seek, Run-Sheep-Run, etc. Sometimes we would sit on the steps of the closed grocery store next door and tell ghost stories. Everyone would have a turn to make up their stories. Some were pretty chilling. After running around, sometimes we were allowed to eat a sandwich before bedtime. Breakfast was usually weak coffee and crackers or bread with butter and jelly. There was no fussing about the food. We ate what was there. After I had Home Ec, Mom was interested in what I had learned so, once in a while, I would cook something that we had tried in class, for instance, creamed peas. Mom liked them but no one else did. When I started to read recipes, I made muffins thinking they were the same as cupcakes so I disappointed my brothers there. Gradually, I learned how to bake layer cakes after conferring with my friend's older sister. She explained a lot and got me a Royal Baking Powder Cookbook. Since Mom liked cake, she had me buy some layer cake pans and the various ingredients we didn't have around the house. (The only baking she did was homemade bread as she did not read or write). The shortening used was lard. The cakes were three layers and butter was used in the icing. I tried a lot of different recipes and everyone looked forward to Saturday when I would bake a cake, sometimes two. My brother bragged about the good cakes I made. Sometimes, they would give a friend a sample.

I enjoyed playing softball in the schoolyard during the summer when a lot of the neighborhood kids got together. We didn't have any equipment but a ball and bat. We caught the ball barehanded and I have some crooked fingers to prove it. When we were in our teens, my brother and I went on hikes with the group of girls next door. They didn't mind us going along. We took our lunch and did a lot of hiking.

Some of the farms on the outskirts of North Dayton would hire kids to pick strawberries during the season. Mom thought I could make some money so one of my friends that knew how to get to the farm said she would show us the way. It was quite a hike to get there and unfortunately the best berries had been picked. They paid three cents a quart for picking. I worked for a long time and all I could find was five quarts of berries in the rows assigned to me. So fifteen cents and a bad case of sunburn was all I had to show for it when I got home. I never went back. I was blistered for weeks.

When I was sixteen, one of my friends told me about the dress shop that hired anyone that said they were over eighteen, to sew. So several of us went there after school was out. The man who did the hiring, asked me my birth date and I already had that figured out so I told him. I was hired and put on sewing belts. The jobs were all piecework, no hourly rate. If the inspector found any bad places, you had to rip them out and redo them on your own time. This was a sweatshop. It was downtown on a second floor and did it ever get hot! Lots of women fainted. My best week netted me $3.23. Right after that, NLRB (the wage law) went into effect with $12 a week minimum. So naturally anyone that couldn't make $12 a week doing piecework was laid off. The girl I had gone there with was fast and good so she made it.

In my sophomore year, someone came around during our study period, asking for volunteers to work in the cafeteria (our study period was during lunch periods). The pay, I believe, was $1 a week. My friend and I went to work. We cleaned tables, scraped, wiped and served. It was fun and we made friends with older students working there. I stayed with it until I graduated and earned a few extra nickels putting up the menu and running the cash register in my senior year. We took silly remarks from other kids for working there but it didn't bother me. The money went a long way toward buying a few clothes. The two cooks were very nice and gave us leftover desserts sometimes. One male teacher liked gravy so well, he asked us to pour it over all the items on his tray. We didn't believe him at first but learned to honor his request. Gravy on pie!

I went to a few football games, home games, on Saturday afternoons but didn't care for them. The animosity and competitiveness between teams was unbelievable, name-calling, rock throwing and fist fighting. We got lectures from the principal during assemblies.

I made the honor roll and made the National Honor Society in my junior year. Of course that meant a speech in front of the whole school. I was petrified but managed to get it done. I still remember standing on the stage trying not to see any of the students sitting in the audience. I had great admiration for those kids who could get up there and not get scared. We had one young man who could play every instrument and he was always performing flawlessly, nothing bothered him. On the whole, I liked most of my teachers with the exception of one junior English teacher. She was a snob and looked down on some of the other teachers. Also in class, she would make caustic remarks to some students when they didn't meet her expectations. I had a home economics teacher who was the opposite. She was always complimenting students on how they looked or on something they had done, always smiling. That meant a lot to some of us. I had a very nice teacher in first grade and was surprised to find her teaching shorthand and typing at high school. She was my teacher and I was happy to see her again.

When I chose the business course to follow, one of the eighth grade teachers told me I should take college prep. She was so emphatic! I tried to tell her that I couldn't finance college and was preparing for office work. Finally she gave up on changing my mind.

It was a shock to me when after my sixteenth birthday, my mother told me that I wasn't going back to school. She said it was time for me to go to work and pay for my "room and board," also she would not buy any schoolbooks. Of course I was stunned. My first thought was *where could I go to get a job?* Lots of adults were still out of work because of the Depression and only experienced workers got hired. I pleaded for her to change her mind but she insisted that was the way it was going to be. I told her I would borrow the books I needed, etc. Finally, my father told her that I probably couldn't get a job and it would be better if I went to school and graduated. He usually let her make the decisions on things concerning the children. I was so relieved!

Thinking back about my childhood, I didn't mind not having the material things, as I knew I could get along without them. The things that mattered were having to "battle" so much about going to school or doing a few things I would like to have done. I did learn to make the best of the situations that came up and enjoyed the things I was allowed to do. It is hard to write about the experiences that impressed me so much that I can still visualize the "scenes" and make others see it as it really happened. It would take reams of paper. I could write a book!

My brother Joe was not quite two years older than me. For the first born to be a son was a feather in the father's cap and the son was treated royally. A girl meant she would get married and the parents would not expect any help from her in their old age but the sons were expected to take care of their parents, if needed. Joe was permitted to "run" around with his friends when he got old enough to know his way around. He got a job delivering newspapers when he was around twelve but didn't have it long. He seemed to lose his money and Mom had to pay for the papers. It was discovered by one of his friend's mothers that he was treating his buddies to ice cream and other goodies. When he got a little older, he and some of his friends did some caddying on the golf links and made some good money. One summer, he earned over $100 and was permitted to buy a used movie projector from a real movie house. He was interested in radios and learned to repair them. He was also good in basketball but didn't like school. I believe he was in his junior year that his grades got so bad he wanted me to do some of his homework but it didn't help. He failed and quit school and went to work in a factory. It wasn't long before he bought a car and the garage had to be extended. I don't believe I rode in it but once.

He and his best friend were always on the go. They usually went to dances in small towns and got acquainted with the girls. His friend had a reputation as a womanizer and drank quite a bit.

Joe started to date a girl and got married at nineteen. They both were young and didn't work on their marriage at all. They had rented a furnished apartment and had to move because they didn't pay the rent (she was seventeen). However, she would go to a credit-clothing store and buy herself an outfit. She wore it daily until she got tired of it and then got another. Needless to say, they wound up in debt. I thought marriage was romantic and when they moved I would visit now and then to see what it was like. She would take in a movie and leave him a note to make his own supper, which was old baloney in the icebox. When she became pregnant, my mother got concerned and would send me over there to see if all was well. She started to get acute pains in her stomach and side and I told Joe to get her to a doctor. He took her to a doctor who told her it was just a part of being pregnant. When she didn't get any better he took her to another doctor and he called the ambulance and had her in the hospital and operated right away. She had appendicitis and barely made it. She lost the five months along baby. My parents took Joe and his wife into their home and looked after his wife until she got well. She finally got a divorce. Later, several years later, we heard through the grapevine she had a son she name Joe, Jr. After a long time, Joe admitted to Mom that he could be his son. I really don't believe Joe was ever financially responsible and that his ex-wife's parents reared him. I don't remember how old Joe was when he went into business for himself as a radio repairman. He had gone into business with a friend as a partner but it didn't work out. He married again and had a wife who worked and they bought a double house and he worked out of his home. She was divorced and had two sons but the sons lived with a relative, maybe the father. She was a nice person and really did everything she could for Joe but it didn't work out and she divorced him. He was not a responsible person. After that, I lost track of him.

My mother always tried to help him out with money, etc. but he told his friends his family didn't care about him. He was always going to doctors for various ailments and had debts all over town. It really is sad he wasn't capable of taking responsibility for his actions.

My younger brother and I had an alliance against my mother when she got after us. He was less than two years younger and we thought alike. When he would get into trouble I would comfort him. Mom always told us to never go near the river by ourselves. One day, Joe convinced him to go swimming in the river. My younger brother didn't know how to swim. When Mom discovered them gone, she got all the neighbors to help search. They finally found them at the river. He got a terrible beating and Joe got put in the closet (he was afraid of the dark). My younger brother went to his bedroom, really sobbing his heart out. I went up to him to see if I could help and he was ready to run away. I convinced him it would be the wrong thing to do. He had a job sorting rotten potatoes and made a little money. He was always willing to share with me and paid for some books. After he quit school at sixteen years old, he got a job at a grocery store and then at the pie company. One time, he decided he wanted to learn to play the accordion and bought a used one and signed up for lessons. However, he gave it up and signed over the balance of the lessons to me. I must have been a junior in high school. I took the lessons and learned to play somewhat. I was no natural born musician but I got satisfaction out of it, and on Sundays, Pop would like to have me play.

When World War II started, my younger brother was put in the First Infantry Division. Their division was among the first to land. He got malaria and had a rough time. To this day, he doesn't like to talk about the war as he lost many of his best friends. I believe he was in radio communication. I always wrote to him and was glad when the war was over.

My next younger brother had his own friends when he was growing up, so as a result, we weren't very close. He liked tinkering with cars so left school and worked as a mechanic. Later went to the factory. He was a marine in the Pacific during World War II.

Stanley was the youngest so I was a second mother to him. I bought him toys and helped him with school. He was a very pleasant child and looked after Mom and Pop when they got old. He was sent to Korea as a medic.

Chapter 38: Maturing

I am my "mother's daughter." It's funny, but as a teen that would have insulted me. I would have associated all the negative qualities I assigned to my mother. I would have labeled myself weak and overly emotional. I would have said neurotic and phobic. But now, knowing the circumstances as I do, I see things so differently. Thinking of the pain she suffered, the incredible patience she showed, I wonder how she made it through this life so well, how she continued to endure with so little support, to carry on day in and day out without feeling that she was loved. She actually showed so much strength, the quiet and enduring kind. Yes, she had her neuroses, she had her problems, but in spite of it all, it was minor compared to what she had to deal with. If only I could have seen it then I wonder how different it would be now.

Someone told me that if you don't see something that is going on, then you weren't meant to and it is not your burden. Perhaps I couldn't do anything to help my mother and perhaps I wasn't supposed to because her life was her lesson to learn. But I still ache for how alone she must have felt.

So being my mother's daughter entails being strong, being there for the long haul, not caving in. What I remember about my mother is her kindness for the downtrodden. She would never kick someone when they were down. She believed in honesty and the lies she told she felt were necessary, to protect us, and was torn apart by guilt for it. She had heart. She felt that treating others with kindness, respect, and caring were the cornerstones of life. For some reason, there was a disconnection about how she could believe this for others but have problems using this with her own children.

Once, a young man's car broke down in front of my parent's house. The young man, poorly dressed and nervous, asked to use the phone. My mother openly asked him into the house and chattered away to him, embracing him in her warmth. After he had gotten his car running and was getting ready to leave, he told my mother that he had been going through a rough spell, with arrests and drugs. A chill ran down my spine to think what could have happened to her, alone in her house with a desperate man, and it didn't occur to her until later what she had done, going against common sense not to let a stranger into her house. I believe that whatever the man had planned was changed by the fact that my mother was openly accepting of him. If he did have sinister plans, they were changed because of her. That is the kind of person she was.

I see her in my dreams at night and at times feel her near me. I know she is free and better off than when on this earth, but if I live to be her age when she died, I will have lived a long time without her. Such a long time, a very long time.

If there is one thing I've learned, it's that there is always hope, there are always miracles waiting around the corner. The pain we all suffer in life is often chosen and we must chose to live life fully. I want to live the legacy of kindness that my mother left behind, to help others the way she did by being a caring, gentle person, to live up to her expectations of me, not only from when she was alive but in the way she can communicate with me now. That means I have to be open to the unknown and listen to my intuition. I want to be able to feel not only her presence, but also her thoughts.

She told me several times in the past few years that I should be a writer. That meant a lot to me to hear her say that and it gives me courage to know that she is up there watching me write this now. And isn't it ironic that the motivation to write is also because of her and the experience of her passing over. Life is full of ironies.

I do believe that her spirit lives on, her energy surrounds me. I can recall what her energy feels like and then I feel such an aching in my chest because of the longing. She used to tell me that sometimes she would wake up in the middle of the night, thinking someone had called out, "Mom!" and she would wonder which one of her children needed her. This was after we were all grown up and had moved away. If I would think about her for a day or so, I would always get a telephone call from her and vice versa. Often, she would be on my mind and I knew I just had to call her. There was a sort of telepathy going on between us and I know it also occurred between her and at least one of my brothers. So, underneath all the day-to-day stuff we went through, there was still an undercurrent of connection.

Chapter 39: Thomas' Own Words

Surprisingly, my dad seemed to enjoy writing this and then talked for hours about his memories. I got the impression that with some of the events he talked about, he almost thought he would be met with disapproval.

Thomas writes:

I know that I have often wished that I had more knowledge of my grandparents. Guess I should have spent some time talking to my Grandpa Readnower but, in my younger days, I wasn't interested in family background. My maternal grandparents died while my mother was a teenager so she lived with an older sister. About all I know about those grandparents is that they lived on a farm in Kentucky and raised two sons and four daughters that included my mother, Anna. I've been told that my maternal grandfather was pretty good at making furniture. Without power tools, making furniture would not be an easy task!

Grandpa and Grandma, on my father's side, lived on a farm at Stringtown, just a crossroads area with a small store that sold kerosene (later gasoline), some food items, tobacco items, rifle and shotgun shells and not much else. The store was owned by the choir director for the church. Church attendance was a social event as well as a religious event. He made and drank wine, which was frowned upon, by a lot of my relatives in that area. When I lived with Red and Rena, she often would send me to the store for a few items. Usually, she let me have a nickel for a Milky Way. I sure loved those candy bars. Also, she would sometimes tell me to get a dime's worth of cheese and crackers. The crackers were not packaged, just stored loose in a bin. The cheese was wrapped in foil and kept in a small wooden box (no refrigeration). The owner would slice off a few pieces of cheese and put it in a brown paper bag with a handful of crackers for a dime. I don't know how the cheese stayed fresh or maybe we just didn't know what fresh cheese was.

The store owner had to pick up his supplies at the train depot in Corinth, a trip of four or five miles. He drove a spring wagon with two black mares. That was quite a sight for a youngster since farm wagons were much larger, had no springs, and usually had little or no paint. That painted spring wagon with two high stepping black mares was a sight worth seeing! But I'm sure it was a long, cold trip in bad weather.

Grandpa and Grandma had three children. Ruby, Rena and my dad. Mother and Dad grew up in the same neighborhood in rural Kentucky. Mother married and had one son, my half-brother Bernard who was twelve years old when I was born. My dad was married and his first wife died (in childbirth, I believe) leaving him with a girl, my half-sister, who was raised by my grandparents, and was about the same age as Bernard. Later, my mom and dad were married and had two children. Mid was first and I was born four years later. I understand I was somewhat of a surprise! A few months after I was born, the family moved to a farm about sixty miles south of Cincinnati. The farm was near a crossroads area, which had a small general store, a church, a school and several farmhouses. That part is hilly land and very little of it is suitable for cultivation. It's marginal farmland but it does grow a lot of bluegrass and is suitable for raising sheep or other grass-eating animals. Farmers in that area also grew small tobacco crops that are labor intensive and require little acreage for a cash crop.

Dad's farm was of average size for the area when we moved there (less than 100 acres) but he added to it thru the years so that when I was a teenager the farm had 309 acres. It was sold when I was in my mid twenties and my folks moved back to the city for a second time.

I spent my early years with several aunts and uncles close by and I was the only grandson so I got lots of attention. I spent a lot of time with my aunt and uncle who had only one child, a girl about Mid's age, whose eventual husband became my hunting companion during high school years. I was also with another aunt and uncle a lot where I also got a lot of attention since they had no children. But most of my time away from home was spent with Aunt Rena and Uncle Red who loved children but had none of their own. From a very early age, I was at their house every time I got a chance. Aunt Rena had been a schoolteacher before marriage and Red was just a big "redneck" farmer that everybody liked. He sure had a strong influence on me.

People who lived and farmed in the area around Stringtown were religious and most attended the Stringtown Christian Church. My grandparents, however, attended the Baptist church. The grandparents did not believe in card playing, dancing or use of alcohol but they were not as strict or dour as that may sound. By present day standards, they were poor people but I doubt very much if they thought of themselves as poor. They had a small farm and raised sheep, chickens and cows. They had large gardens and grew all of their food. The four or five cows provided lots of milk and butter and some cash income from the sale of milk/cream and calves. The sheep provided some income from the sale of lambs and wool. They also raised a few hogs each year that were butchered for meat. Almost all of the meat in their diet was chicken or pork. Grandad also kept honeybees and sold honey. My grandparent's house was small (five rooms) and heated by individual wood burning stoves. Every room, except the kitchen, had a bed in it. Grandma wore long dresses, mostly dark colors, with long sleeves and her hair piled on the back of her head. In those days, women did not cut their hair. Grandpa wore bib overalls and I can't remember ever seeing him with his sleeves rolled up. He was inclined to become exasperated at times and when he did, Grandma just went about her work singing religious songs. It's hard to have an argument with someone that just sings!

Grandpa was very respected in the community but was not a prosperous farmer. Their home would most likely be called a shack by today's standards but it was typical of the farmhouses in that area. It was small and had a metal roof that was noisy when it rained. When I was small, my uncle and Aunt Ruby moved to the city where he worked in a Ford plant. When the depression of the early thirties hit, he was laid off and they decided to move back to their little farm. The farmhouse of four rooms had deteriorated through the years so while it was being fixed up, my uncle, my aunt and my cousin, her husband and their son all moved in with Grandpa and Grandma. I'm sure they were crowded, but in those days welfare was a dirty word, if it existed at all, and families had to look out for each other. After the house was repaired, they all moved back to their own home. Again a bed in every room, except the kitchen.

The lives of the people who lived in that rural area were all about the same. Lots of hard work but they helped each other with the heavy farm work. Dad and Mother were the prosperous ones, although by our present day standards they were certainly not rich.

Dad had worked for a life insurance company and had a disability policy that paid very well after he became disabled. He had a series of disablements, the last of which was an accident with a shotgun that took his left hand and the front half of his left foot. After that, or rather shortly before, he got interested in tracing the family tree, etc. I had to drive for him and I sure got tired of that chore. We must have driven thousands of miles for him to interview people and examine old records.

While I was little and lived on the farm, I had lots of pets. A big dog, Bepo, who died when our house burned down, rabbits, a goat and a pony. Grandpa bought a mare pony for my half sister and then raised three colts. The first was for my cousin since she was the oldest, the next was for Mid and the third was for me.

I can remember Dad bringing the dog home in a shoebox when he was just a little pup. When I was about five years old, our house caught fire while we were at church. Someone saw the blaze and came to the church for Dad. Practically the entire male congregation went to help put out the fire but it was too late. Everything burned, including my dog.

The goat was given to me by Red and Rena when I was about three or four years old. They put the goat in a large turkey shed for the night. Next morning, someone suggested that I go get the goat. It was a young female and not too big. I opened the front of the pen. The goat, which probably was scared, saw daylight and came running out past me. The goat ran around the back of the house with me in hot pursuit, and yelling for help. My mother and an aunt came out and they captured the goat. Needless to say, the goat and I became great friends. They really are nice pets and the females don't have a strong odor like males.

The two rabbits I had met an untimely end when someone neglected to secure their cage for the night and a cat got to them. While I had them, I played with them inside the house and they ate the green straw out of a rug Mother had in one room. Things like that didn't upset her since she never saw an animal she didn't like.

The goat eventually hung herself. She had horns that wound back over her head. She was in a lot with a wire fence. She rose up on her hind feet and pushed her head through the fence to nibble on some green apple-tree leaves. When she tried to get down, the horns caught in the wire fence and she strangled. That's the way we found her, which was another black day in my young life.

My pony was a male (light tan) Shetland, so his name was Bay Beauty. He was a spirited but lovable pony and I rode him for many a mile. After our house burned, we moved back to the city but I spent the summers with Red and Rena. Dad still kept his farm and the ponies stayed there during the school season. When I arrived after school was out, I couldn't wait to get the pony back to Red's farm. For the summer season, the pony had to be shod with steel shoes to protect his feet. He didn't exactly like that idea so sometimes Red postponed the process longer than he should have. I can remember one summer in which the pony's feet became somewhat tender because of no shoes. As a result, when I would enter the lot with a bridle, the pony would lay back his ears, run toward me and just before it got too close, would turn and kick at me with both hind feet. That was a little unnerving for a seven or eight-year-old boy! Dad and Red saw it happen and proceeded to tell me not to be afraid. In fact, they said, stand your ground and when the pony turns to kick, step close and whack him with the bridle reins. I wasn't at all sure that would work but if those two said it would, I was willing to try. Lo and behold, it did work, the pony cut out that nonsense and we had a great summer. Red soon got the shoes on the pony, but until he did, I tried to ride him only on grassy areas.

The pony was a rotund animal and so I often rode him without a saddle for short trips. His broad back made a comfortable seat. On one such occasion, I rode him to the store for Aunt Rena. One the way home I had several grocery items in my arms, the bridle reins were lying loosely on the pony's neck, my feet were dangling (no saddle), the sun was shining brightly and neither the pony nor I had a care in the world. Suddenly, a large German shepherd jumped out of the weeds and barked at the pony's heels. The pony kicked at the dog with both hind feet and me and the groceries went off onto the rock road. The dog ran away and the pony went trotting on home. Red saw the pony come home alone and was starting out to look for me when I came trudging into view with what was left of the groceries. I really didn't think I was hurt until Red saw blood flowing from the back of my head. He went and got Dad who was out at our farm and the two of them decided I should see a doctor. So we went to see the doctor who worked the cut with alcohol and took a couple of stitches. I almost passed out during that procedure.

Another episode from my childhood took place while we still lived on the farm. Dad had a team of mules and on this particular day he and a hired hand brought the team to the house to get water from the cistern. After they had their fill of water, the hired hand led one mule back to the barn area. Dad was going to lead the other one but first he put me on the mule for a ride to the barn. We were about halfway to the barn when my hat blew off and hit the mule on the rump. That scared the mule and it took off! I landed unhurt and my first statement was, "Don't tell Mom!" She didn't think her small son (less than five years old) should be riding mules! She didn't find out until years later what had happened but she apparently knew something was wrong since I wasn't very lively or hungry for lunch. I often wonder how farm kids survive.

I guess any discussion of my childhood would not be complete without some comments about school. In that rural area, one-room schoolhouses with one teacher handling grades one through eight were all that existed. The school was heated with a big wood-burning stove. Water for drinking was from a cistern. A bucket of water was kept in the schoolhouse with a dipper for all to use. If we ever washed our hands, I don't remember it. I'm sure there were no towels. There was a woodshed to keep the lots dry and an outhouse with separate sides for boys and girls. The teacher was boarded at our house during the week since her home was in Corinth and the road was terrible in bad weather. Before I started to school, she used to play with me a lot and told Mother that she somewhat dreaded the day I would start to school since she didn't know just how she could control her little rowdy playmate. However, there was no problem. The school was just a short distance from our farm home. Before the first year was out, the house burned and we moved into an empty farmhouse at Stringtown that was owned by an aunt. From there I went to Stringtown School that was another one room school. The farmhouse was empty because my aunt's husband had died and she moved to Covington and purchased a rooming house where she lived and rented out apartments and rooms. She must have been a pretty smart businesswoman since she parlayed her earnings into a second place and then a third. At some point, she remarried a man who was a handyman and pretty good with tools. Maybe that ability made him more attractive to her since he certainly wasn't very handsome. However, he was a nice person.

We only lived at the house in Stringtown a short time and then we moved back to Covington in a three-room apartment over a grocery store. There was also an unheated room in the attic where my brother and his cousin lived for a short time.

In the one room schoolhouse environment, I progressed to the fourth grade even though by age I was only old enough for first grade. This was largely because the teacher worked with Mid and I and advanced us in grades without regard to age. When I entered school in Covington, I was quickly returned to first grade. I think I might have been able to do the work at a higher grade but, I, as a young farm boy, was intimidated by the large school and more kids than I had ever seen. That old school was three stories high with oiled wooden floors and only two restrooms. The floors were a definite fire hazard! The restrooms were in the basement with entrances from outside. The schoolyard was divided into two parts with the boys and girls separated by the building. At one end of the building was a fire escape, which consisted of a large, completely enclosed circular structure with an entrance at the second and third floors.

Inside, it was like a huge playground slide, only completely dark. Fire drills, during which we had to enter that contraption and slide down to the ground level, were not something I liked. I stayed in that school through the fifth grade. By the time I was ready for high school, I had attended four different schools.

In the meantime, Mid stayed in Corinth with our original teacher until she finished the eighth grade. She finished high school when she was fifteen.

After we moved to Covington, I spent the summer with Red and Rena. They didn't believe in much discipline and Red took me with him everywhere he went. Dad and another uncle still had their farms and Red looked after them for a part of the farm income. Dad's farm raised sheep with wool to sell in the spring and lambs to sell in summer and there were many acres of hay to be harvested for winter feed for the sheep. Periodically, the sheep had to be rounded up, counted and checked for any problems. In doing this, I rode the pony and Red rode a bay mare called Old Nell. We rode many miles looking for stray sheep or cattle. Several times Dad tried raising cattle. He would buy young cattle and fatten them on grain during the summer and sell them in the fall. The idea was to buy young ones, let them grow on grass that was plentiful and sell them for a profit. Unfortunately, the market price didn't always cooperate. The price per pound in the fall might well be lower than the spring price so profits from cattle in the area were rather poor. But in the meantime, Red and I chased the cattle and sheep. I'm sure it was lots of work for him (but for me it was lots of fun). The pony could outrun the mare so whenever we had any races (which were frequent) Red would get a head start by surprise. He would yell something like, "Beat you to the next gate," and be off and gone before I knew what was going on. The pony was fast and we usually caught him pretty quickly. I guess it was fun things like that, that made me enjoy his company.

I remember one extremely hot day he suggested we take off our clothes and go in the creek. The creek wasn't very deep, but the water was cool and we were having fun splashing around. Red was afraid of snakes and about the time our fun was going well, a water snake came swimming across the water. I'm sure the snake was harmless but I can still see Red standing naked in the middle of the creek saying, "Oooh, there's a snake." That finished our fun for that day. I guess my dislike of snakes may stem in part from Red's reaction to snakes. He killed every one he could.

Another event that I will always remember might well be called the "Case of the Lovesick Stud Horse." Red and Rena raised a few turkeys each year and the young ones were sold in late fall. During the summer, the young ones and the old hens roosted at night in a large tree in the back yard. During the day, they roamed the fields eating bugs and seeds. On one occasion, they roamed too far and failed to come home at night. Next morning, Red and I set out to find the turkeys. Red was riding the bay mare and I was on the pony. We had some trouble locating the turkeys and eventually entered a neighbor's farm pasture to look for them. The pasture was quite large and we were well into it when we realized that the neighbor's horses, including a stud, were also in the pasture. Male horses are not easy to control and when they see a strange mare, they become practically unmanageable and sometimes downright mean. The stud saw the mare from a distance and came toward us at a fast trot. When we saw him, it was too late to get out of the pasture. Red assured me that the stud wouldn't hurt the pony but told me to keep well away from the mare. He dismounted and picked up a fairly large club that just happened to be available. He then got back in the saddle. By then, the stud arrived with sex on his mind. He attempted to mount the mare with Red still in the saddle. This procedure brought the stud's nose and big teeth pretty close to Red's back. He turned and whacked the stud on the nose with the club about as hard as he could. That sure took the love light out of the stud's eyes. By the time he regained his composure, we were out of the pasture. The course of true love doesn't always run smoothly even for horses. I still don't remember finding those darn turkeys.

Red and Rena raised chickens, turkeys, sheep, cows and a few hogs. At an early age, I learned to milk a cow, feed the pigs or the orphaned lambs. Each year, there would be three or four orphaned lambs that had to be fed milk from a bottle with a large nipple on it. Red also had two horses. One was strictly a draft animal used in a team with Grandpa's mare. The other was Old Nell, the bay mare. She was quite gentle and I wanted to be able to jump on her back without a saddle like the grown ups could. It was a big achievement when I finally accomplished it after many attempts. When Red was going to use the bay mare, I would take the bridle and go after her in the pasture, then ride her back to the barn. On one occasion, when I approached with the bridle, both horses decided they didn't want to work that day and proceeded to walk away. I tried my best to corner them but couldn't and finally had to go back to the house and tell Red I couldn't catch either horse. He came back with me but by then both horses were determined not to be caught. Finally, we got them cornered where two fences met. Red was equally determined. As they tried to get out of the corner, Red would step in front of them while talking to them in a soothing voice. Finally, the black mare, which we didn't want, managed to escape by jumping down a steep bank and across a small stream. The bay was alone and soon calmed down so Red could get the bridle on her and we both rode her back to the barn.

Another episode concerns an uncle and me and the barn roof. It was while my uncle was visiting at Aunt Rena's house. He wanted to do some repair work on his barn and I wanted to go with him. When we got to the barn, he proceeded to climb up on the roof to work and I climbed up with him. I was just a little guy at the time so I guess he shouldn't have let me get up on the roof but he did. Red happened to be about a half mile away at Dad's farm. He looked in our direction, saw me on the barn roof and about had heart failure. He put the mare into a fast lope and got me off the roof with no damage done. Like I said before, it's a wonder kids on a farm even grow to adulthood.

When the Stringtown Christian Church was destroyed by fire, it was rebuilt with most of the funds provided by my aunt. She had only one son, who I am told, was pretty wild in his younger days. He married and had one boy who, at an early age, became crippled physically and mentally and died when he was just a little boy. His father had contracted syphilis. This caused the boy's problems. The father also deteriorated mentally and died at an early age. I'm sure this was a great disappointment to my aunt.

My half brother, Bernard, married and had four children. One died while just a baby. My half-sister married and had three sons, one of whom died when about sixteen. He had a heart defect not known until after his death. He died on the way home from school and his father found him by the roadside.

Chapter 40: Making Sense

What is it that makes people do the things they do? Instead of watching someone make choices and see it happen in real time, I've had to go back sixty years and try to piece together all the little puzzles that were my parents and aunt and uncle. I've had to try and figure out all the little twists and turns that were their lives and wonder.... would their lives have been different if the events of 1947 and before didn't happen? How would *MY* life have been different?

Never make waves, never speak up, never be seen, just keep your head down and be a good girl. Be traditional, don't be TOO smart, don't attract attention, don't have ambition. Marry someone to be taken care of, stay where you are, don't get ahead of yourself, be normal... Those are the words that echoed in my life growing up, mostly silently, but definitely echoing through the forces of my life just as if it was an element in the air that I breathed. Its energy was suffocating, attempting to squash me into a box that I didn't ever belong in. It was as though there was a silent, still prison wrapped around me.

But what if... what if I would have been told about the secrets, about the past that no one dared share with me? What if I could have looked upon the family as having wounds that just wouldn't heal so that I could understand more readily their feelings of wanting to keep us hidden from the tribulations of the world? Would it have been different for me? Could I have looked at my family with wistfulness, but seen their actions as a form of post traumatic stress and then carried on as though it didn't affect me? I could have been a soldier who carried on and did what needed to be done and all the while "protected" the family from its pain and shame. I would have been more patient, more understanding, more worldly in my actions. I wouldn't have been blindsided later in life and realized that everything I was told was a lie, a big fat, stinking lie.

So there you go, my life laid bare. In telling this, I tell you my secrets, my family's secrets and am completely vulnerable. It's completely scary, infinitely embarrassing and I alternate between holding my head up proudly and wanting to slink into the background with my tears. But if nothing else, whatever emotion you feel, let this be a subtle cautionary tale of what unspoken secrets can do to you.

Epilogue

My dad lived five years after my mother passed over, spending his days, every day with Lydia. I think she kept him alive. He seemed to want my blessing for the relationship and I freely gave it. One time, a very awkward moment for me, he discussed going to the doctor and getting a prescription for Viagra. Yikes, did I really have to hear that? Later, he told me precisely, "For your information, the Viagra didn't work." Okay, Dad, I wasn't asking.

He refused to marry Lydia, although that is what she wanted, even offering to sign a pre-nup. He also refused to tell her why they never married nor even discuss it with her. He didn't want to tell her that once my mother showed up in his life, no one else could hope to capture his eye. Whatever was between my mother and father, I will never truly and completely understand. Their relationship was complicated and full of twists and turns.

In his last years, my father was mellow, finally saying the things I longed to hear as a child… how much he loved me, how proud he was of me, how much he wanted me to be happy and that I was the pride of his life. He wanted to hug, a lot!

His final days were spent in and out of hallucinations where he kept accusing the doctors of being "the scoundrel," taking me back to those days of World War II just by the term "scoundrel" and wondering if he was back there too. Had he returned in his mind to those days of scandal and notoriety? Was he reliving it all in his mind?

I sat at his bedside and held his hand. It seemed to be the only thing that calmed him down. If I left the room, he would call out for me to run back in and take my seat again. He held on tightly and I talked and talked, taking him back to the countryside where he grew up, picturing the green pastures and streams, his beloved uncle and aunt and the animals he loved. That seemed to give him comfort.

By a twist of fate, I was alone in the room with him when he passed. We knew the time was coming by the pauses in his breathing and the coldness of his feet. The nurses told us what to watch for. At the precise moment, I stood by his bedside, my hand on his arm, his breath suspended. I waited, as though time stood still. His eyes moved, opened wider and it was as if I could see into his core. He looked straight at me with eyes that spoke of the ages, of life and death, of the spirit that had resided within his body and was now getting ready to fly away. With a final whoosh of his breath, his eyes returned to normal, and he was gone. I know that I was given a gift, to see the true consciousness within him, and that is something I will never forget.

Appendix- Photo Gallery

Mom (Kathryn) -1940's

Dad (1940's) in Uniform

Bler Lamarre, California 1939

Mildred (Mid) Lamarre

Dad, his Mom and Dad, Rena and Red

Mid, Age 15, High School Graduation

Mom and Me

Mid and Me

Bler and Dad

Mid and Her Collie

Mid and Bler in Later Years

Mom and Dad Fifty Year Anniversary

About The Author

Cynthia Readnower, M.B.A., is a certified life coach, writer and publisher. Her career has spanned corporate positions in sales and marketing, restaurant ownership, entrepreneurship and being a stay at home mom. She has been a regular columnist for a local paper for over ten years and has won two awards for Sarasota's Favorite Life Coach. She has appeared on local television, Internet television, and radio.

Her interests lie in investigating the mysteries of life.

Bibliography

"Mate Of 'Borrowed' Love Says Officer Smears Him, Wife to Beat Fraud Count." *The Dayton Journal* 22 Nov. 1947 Front Page: Print

Foglietta, Tony. "Parents Brand Love Story 'Lie'." *The Dayton Journal* 22Nov. 1947 Front Page: Print

Nathan, Maxwell. "Meyers To Face Slander Action, Journal-Herald Given Exclusive Interview With Mrs. Lamarre: Attractive Brunet Labels Testimony 'Barefaced Lies'. " The Dayton Journal 24 Nov. 1947 Front Page: Print

Spargo, Mary. "Gen. Meyers Called Liar And Snake By Lamarre." *The Washington Post* 22 Nov. 1947 Front Page: Print

"Lamarre's Wife Brands Meyers Liar." *The Washington Post* 22 Nov. 1947: Print

"Meyers' In-Laws Questioned." *The Washington Post* 22 Nov. 1947: Print

"Meyers Blames Woes On 'Love', General Declares Fraud, Perjury Charges False." *The Dayton Journal* 21 Nov. 1947 Front Page: Print

"Exclusive: Mildred Lamarre Relates Her Story." *The Dayton Herald* 24 Nov. 1947 Front Page: Print

"Meyers To Face 'New Evidence', Justice Department Prepares To Act." *The Dayton Herald* 24 Nov. 1947 Front Page: Print

Vincent, Jack. "Daytonian To Sue Meyers." *The Dayton Herald* 24 Nov. 1947 Front Page: Print

"What's Guy To Say?" *The Dayton Herald* 24 Nov. 1947 Front Page: Print

Vincent, Jack "Come In, I Want To Talk, Mrs. Lamarre Tells Reporters." *The Dayton Herald* 24 Nov. 1947

"Mrs. Lamarre Tells Story; Plans To Sue General Meyers." *The Dayton Herald* 24 Nov. 1947 Page 2: Print

"Second Wife Charged Meyers With Cruelty." *The Dayton Herald* 24 Nov. 1947: Print

Rosensweet, Alvin. "Where's Mrs. Lamarre? Nobody Answers The Door." *The Dayton Herald* 21 Nov. 1947 Front Page: Print

"Affidavit False, Meyers Admits, General Insists He Wanted To Aid His 'Girl Friend'." *The Dayton Herald* 21 Nov. 1947 Front Page: Print

Brown, Marie Thrailkill. "Aviation Electric Based On Love Affair, Meyers Says." *The Dayton Herald* 21 Nov. 1947 Page 16:Print

"Meyers Firm Records In Dayton, 'Ghost'Haunts Building." *The Dayton Herald* 21 Nov. 1947: Print

"AAF Subcontracting Firm Owned By Gen. Meyers, Testimony Shows." *Aviation Week* 24 Nov. 1947, Vol. 47 No. 21, Page 11:Print

Van Tyne, Edmond. "The Fantastic General Meyers." *True Detective Magazine* June, Pages 12-15, 66-71: Print

Brown, Marie Thrailkill. "Lamarre Denounces Meyers as 'Liar, Snake'. " *The Dayton Herald* 22 Nov. 1947: Print

"Meyers Admits Auto Affidavit False." *The Dayton Daily News* 21 Nov. 1947 Front Page: Print

"Meyers Lied For 'Revenge', Mildred's Mother Tells News." *The Dayton Daily News* 21 Nov. 1947: Print

White, William. "Meyers''Love Affair'Revelations Stun Listeners." *The Dayton Daily News* 21 Nov. 1947 Page 6: Print

"Major General Bennett E. Meyers." U.S. Air Force Public Website, December 2012

Meyers v. United States, United States Court of Appeals of Columbia Circuit No. 9797, Argued 14 June 1948, Decided 8 Nov. 1948, Lexis Nexis.

Bleriot Lamarre Collection 1931-1986. Walter Havighurst Special Collections, Miami University Libraries, online.

Rosensweet, Alvin. "Lamarre Joins Wife At Home On Oakley Ave." *The Dayton Herald* 22 Nov. 1947 Front Page: Print

"Arnold Calls Meyers 'Liar, Disgrace To Uniform'." *The Dayton Herald* 22 Nov. 1947 Front Page: Print

"Wartime Chief Denies Approval Of Stock Deals." *The Dayton Herald* 22 Nov. 1947 Front Page: Print

"Meyers Threatened With Slander Suit." *The Dayton Journal* 24 Nov. 1947 Print

Cull Jr., Dick. "Meyers says Senate Hearing 'Horribly Unfair Presentation'." *The Dayton Daily News* 22 Nov. 1947 Front Page: Print

" 'No Comment', Lamarre Says On Return Here". *The Dayton Daily News* 22 Nov. 1947 Front Page: Print

"Lamarre Wins His Freedom." *The Wisconsin State Journal* 19 March 1949 Online

"Meyers Convicted, Faces 30 Year Term." *The Evening Leader*, Corning, NY 13 March 1948. Front Page: Online

"Probe: Gen. Bennett Meyers, War Record Reviewed." *The Tuscaloosa News* 23 Nov. 1947 Online

"Bennett Meyers Back in Prison, Tax Delinquency Brings Sentence." *The Eugene Register* 11 April 1951: Online

Barlett, Donald L. and Steele, James B. *Howard Hughes: His Life & Madness*, W.W. Norton & Company, Inc. Web. March 2013

"High Court Refuses to Review the Case of Bennett Meyers." The Milwaukee Journal 14 Feb. 1949: Online

"Clark To Ask Indictment Of Meyers On Tax Count, General Profited $150,199 From Plant, Is Charge." *The Portland Press Herald*, Portland, Maine 20 Nov. 1947 Front Page: Online

"Meyers Hearing." *The Hattiesburg American*, Hattiesburg, Mississippi 19 Nov. 1947: Online

"Readnower Salary Went To Meyers, Letter Coverup Blamed On Air Force Leaders." *The Corpus Christi Times*, Corpus Christi, Texas 19 Nov. 1947 Front Page: Online

"Arnold Brands Meyers As Rotten Apple In The Barrel, Terms Him A Liar and Disgrace to Uniform, Rank." *The Lowell Sun*, Lowell, Mass. 22 Nov. 1947 Front Page: Online

" 'I'm Being Made the Goat'–Meyers, Kiss and Tell General Says He Welcomes Probe." The Lowell Sun, Lowell, Mass. 22 Nov. 1947 Front Page: Online

"Service Salary Went to Meyers." *Reno Evening Gazette*, Reno, Nevada 19 Nov. 1947 Front Page: Online

"Meyers Got Most Of His Pay, Firm Officer Declares." *The Daily Inter Lake*, Kalispell, Montana 19 Nov. 1947 Front Page: Online

"Calls Meyers a 'Snake'; Asks He Be Made to Crawl." *Joplin Globe*, Joplin, Missouri 22 Nov. 1947 Front Page: Online

Craig, May. "Inside In Washington." *Portland Press Herald* 25 Nov. 1947 Online

"General Promised Expenses, Plus, Witness Testifies at Meyers Trial." *Nevada State Journal,* Reno, Nevada 5 March 1948 Front Page: Online

"War Probers Told Meyers Padded Rolls, Another 'Executive' Says He Passed His 'Salary' to General." *Oakland Tribune*, Oakland, California 19 Nov. 1947 Online

"War Plant Paid Meyers $94,000, Probers Are Told" *Bridgeport Telegram*, Bridgeport, Connecticut 19 Nov. 1947 Online

"Cash Payments To Meyers Told." *San Antonio Light,* San Antonio, Texas, 5 Oct. 1952 Online

Donovan, James. "Jurors Nearing End Of Probe." *Tucson Daily Citizen*, Tucson, Arizona 4 Dec. 1947 Online

"Arrest Accused Man's Wife, Kentucky Authorities Implicate Vincennes Woman in Murder." *Indianapolis Star* 31 August 1911 Online

"Arrest Wife For Murder, Woman Had Gone To Court To Testify For Second Husband." *The Washington Post* 31 August 1911 Online

"Widow Of Murdered Man and Her Husband Escape By Alibis." *Fort Wayne Journal Gazette* 6 Sept. 1911 Online

"Catches Alleged Murderer." *The Danville Gazette and Mooresville Times* 31 August 1911 Online

www.ingramcontent.com/pod-product-compliance
Lightning Source LLC
Chambersburg PA
CBHW071921290426
44110CB00013B/1437